Editor-in-Chief and Founder:
    Lyndon H. LaRouche, Jr.
Editorial Board: *Lyndon H. LaRouche, Jr. , Helga
    Zepp-LaRouche, Robert Ingraham, Tony
    Papert, Gerald Rose, Dennis Small, Jeffrey
    Steinberg, William Wertz*
Co-Editors: *Robert Ingraham, Tony Papert*
Managing Editor: *Nancy Spannaus*
Technology: *Marsha Freeman*
Books: *Katherine Notley*
Ebooks: *Richard Burden*
Graphics: *Alan Yue*
Photos: *Stuart Lewis*
Circulation Manager: *Stanley Ezrol*

INTELLIGENCE DIRECTORS
Counterintelligence: *Jeffrey Steinberg, Michele
    Steinberg*
Economics: *John Hoefle, Marcia Merry Baker,
    Paul Gallagher*
History: *Anton Chaitkin*
Ibero-America: *Dennis Small*
Russia and Eastern Europe: *Rachel Douglas*
United States: *Debra Freeman*

INTERNATIONAL BUREAUS
Bogotá: *Miriam Redondo*
Berlin: *Rainer Apel*
Copenhagen: *Tom Gillesberg*
Houston: *Harley Schlanger*
Lima: *Sara Madueño*
Melbourne: *Robert Barwick*
Mexico City: *Gerardo Castilleja Chávez*
New Delhi: *Ramtanu Maitra*
Paris: *Christine Bierre*
Stockholm: *Ulf Sandmark*
United Nations, N.Y.C.: *Leni Rubinstein*
Washington, D.C.: *William Jones*
Wiesbaden: *Göran Haglund*

ON THE WEB
e-mail: eirns@larouchepub.com
www.larouchepub.com
www.executiveintelligencereview.com
www.larouchepub.com/eiw
Webmaster: *John Sigerson*
Assistant Webmaster: *George Hollis*
Editor, Arabic-language edition: *Hussein Askary*

EIR (ISSN 0273-6314) *is published weekly
(50 issues), by EIR News Service, Inc.,
P.O. Box 17390, Washington, D.C. 20041-0390.
(703) 297-8434*

European Headquarters: E.I.R. GmbH, Postfach
Bahnstrasse 9a, D-65205, Wiesbaden, Germany
Tel: 49-611-73650
Homepage: http://www.eir.de
e-mail: info@eir.de
Director: Georg Neudecker

Montreal, Canada: 514-461-1557
eir@eircanada.ca

Denmark: EIR - Danmark, Sankt Knuds Vej 11,
basement left, DK-1903 Frederiksberg, Denmark.
Tel.: +45 35 43 60 40, Fax: +45 35 43 87 57. e-mail:
eirdk@hotmail.com.

Mexico City: EIR, Sor Juana Inés de la Cruz 242-2
Col. Agricultura C.P. 11360
Delegación M. Hidalgo, México D.F.
Tel. (5525) 5318-2301
eirmexico@gmail.com

Copyright: ©2017 EIR News Service. All rights
reserved. Reproduction in whole or in part without
permission strictly prohibited.

Canada Post Publication Sales Agreement
#40683579

Postmaster: Send all address changes to *EIR*, P.O.
Box 17390, Washington, D.C. 20041-0390.

Signed articles in *EIR* represent the views of the authors,
and not necessarily those of the Editorial Board.

Cancel the British System, Save the People

EIRContents

www.larouchepub.com Volume 44, Number 33, August 18, 2017

"Cancel the British System, save the people." Lyndon H. LaRouche, Jr. spoke to this effect on July 31. The photo is from Feb. 25, 2012.

LaRouche PAC TV

CANCEL THE BRITISH SYSTEM, SAVE THE PEOPLE

Good and Bad Government, And Citizens' Optimism

by Helga Zepp-LaRouche, chairwoman of the German political party, Civil Rights Movement Solidarity (BüSo)

Aug. 12—Neither the government nor the state has any end other than to dedicate itself to the general welfare— as astonishing as this idea may seem in many countries today. The metric for judging a government is the well-being and happiness of the citizens. In this respect the result of a study by the market research and consulting firm Ipsos is instructive: 87% of the Chinese (aged 16 to 64) who were polled believe that their country is headed in the right direction, while only 42% of the same age group in Germany is of this opinion. To underscore the same point, in China only 13% of the people are pessimistic in that regard, while 58% in Germany are. In the United States only 43% are optimistic, but that is considerably more than a year ago under the Obama administration.

This is not a new subject. As early as 1338-1339, Ambrogio Lorenzetti created a fresco on the effects of good and bad government on the walls of the Council Room (Hall of the Nine) in Siena, Italy. The characteristics of the former are presented in several images: fruitful fields, flourishing trade, relaxed people, and peace; the characteristics of the latter are immortalized in an image as well:

tyranny and the dominance of such vices as greed, arrogance, vanity, cruelty, treason, deception, rage, strife, and war. Justice lies in chains on the ground; the people suffer.

The Current Conflict in the U.S.

To begin with bad government: In an interview with the American blog *Consortium News*, Craig Murray, the British ambassador to Uzbekistan from 2002 to 2004—who quit in protest against the then illegal renditions by the CIA in Uzbekistan—shed light on one

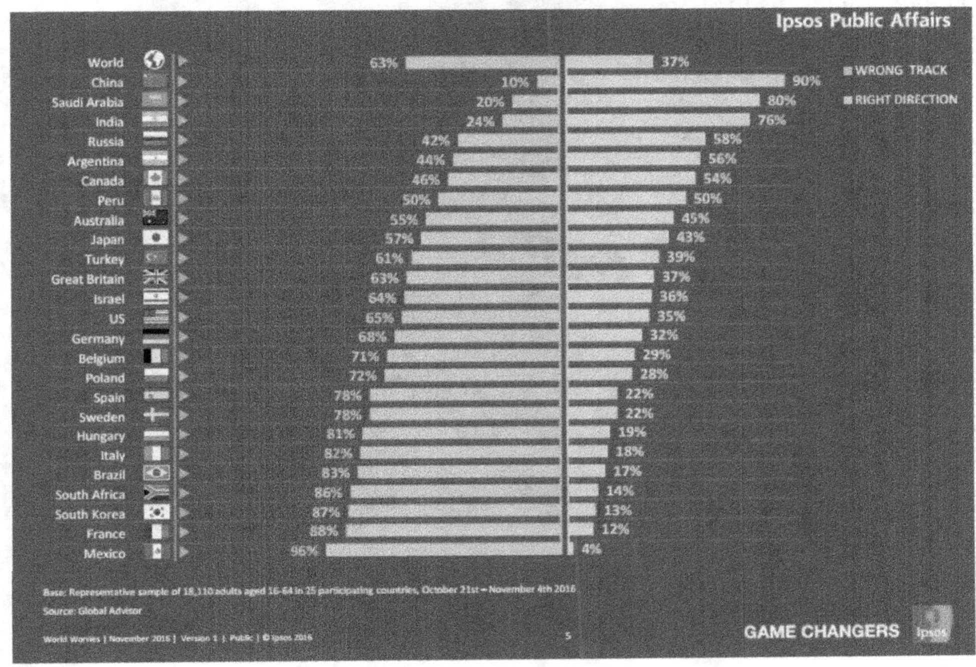

Craig Murray, former British Ambassador to Uzbekistan.

aspect of Anglo-American policy under Tony Blair and George W. Bush, to which the "community of western values" apparently had no objection.

He described how, in his judgment, the testimony of 99% of the people in CIA internment camps in Uzbekistan, who were forced under torture to admit they belonged to al-Qaeda, was worthless. He said that the goal of these operations was to exaggerate the al-Qaeda threat, in order to have an excuse for wars of intervention, as well as for restrictions on human rights in the United States itself. In fact, the famous "whistle-blower" of the 17th Century, Friedrich von Spee, in numerous writings, exposed that confessions made under torture are worthless.

And how should one assess the fact that the Washington newspaper and website *The Hill* simply quotes a CNN interview with the former deputy FBI Director under Robert Mueller, Phil Mudd, that the U.S. government will kill President Trump, because he has set the professionals of the CIA and the State Department against him by defending Putin? No criticism, no outrage—it was just as if the weatherman had forecast rain for tomorrow. Robert Mueller is currently the special prosecutor on Trump's alleged collusion with Russia, and has already empanelled a grand jury, which is supposed to provide the evidence to lead to President Trump's impeachment. It will be interesting to see whether Phil Mudd's announcement will result in an appropriate investigation for having been a signal and a threat against the President by the same intelligence apparat involved in the ongoing coup against the President.

As we go to press, the memorandum by the Veteran Intelligence Professionals for Sanity (VIPS)—who provided forensic proof that there was no so-called hack of the Democratic National Committee's (DNC's) computers by Russia—has gotten international circulation on hundreds of websites in many countries, countless shares on social media, and a breakthrough in mainstream media such as *The Nation*, Fox TV, *Breitbart*, and *Bloomberg News*. Thus the effort by the mainstream media and the neocon establishment to prevent exposure of what is likely to be the greatest scandal in American history, has most likely failed. If there was no Russian hack attack on the DNC's computers, but the email release was an inside operation, that removes the basis for the so-called Russia-gate—and then the spotlight will be directed to the real issue.

The editor of *The Nation*, Katrina van den Heuvel, published a commentary in the *Washington Post* on August 9, "The Emerging Unholy Alliance between Hawkish Democrats and Neoconservatives," in which she exposed what actually lies behind the unprecedented bipartisan vote in both Houses of Congress for new sanctions against

Former FBI Director Robert Mueller (front), the special counsel probing Russian interference in the 2016 U.S. election, after meeting with the Senate Judiciary Committee on Capitol Hill, June 21, 2017.

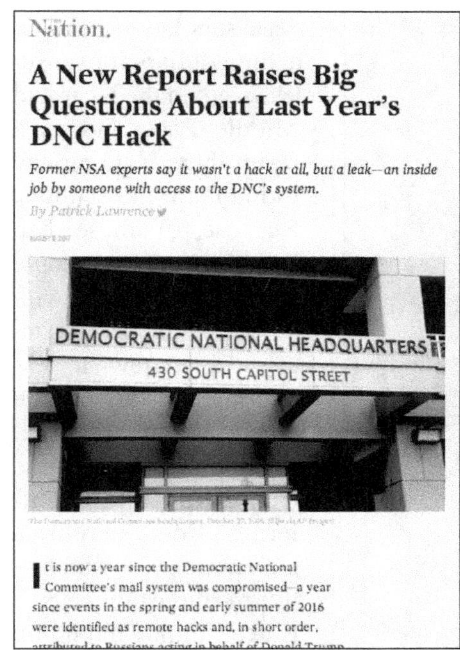

Examples of increased press and Internet coverage of the VIPS exposure of the fraud of the alleged Russian hack of the DNC server.

If, on the other hand, investigations can prove that the entire narrative of apparent collusion between Trump and Russia is a "Brennan Operation" (as eminent journalist Seymour Hersh stresses), then American society will undergo a catharsis tantamount to a second American Revolution. The real collusion is not between Trump and Putin, but between the British and American intelligence services—in their well documented manipulations as they attempt to pull off a coup against the elected President of the United States.

A Change of Scene

On August 11, the *Neue Zürcher Zeitung*, normally the mouthpiece of the Swiss financial institutions, published a remarkable article entitled "China, a Power for Peace?" The author, Junhua Zhang, described in his guest commentary how China, with its Silk Road Project (described as one of the most ambitious programs in human history), has emerged as a new international peacemaker. Wherever there are New Silk Road projects, China has also been engaged in overcoming ethnic and territorial conflict through development and mediation between the conflicting parties, as in Burma, between Pakistan and Afghanistan, between Eritrea and Ethiopia, in South Sudan, and between Israel and Palestine—to name only a few.

This beneficial result flows naturally from all the investments in railroad lines, industrial parks, hydroelectric dams, agricultural development, and the rest, which, as part

Russia (and Iran and North Korea). It is a new edition of the neocon project of 1997, the Project for a New American Century, under which the United States and Great Britain claim the right to impose a unipolar world—based on the Anglo-American special relationship. The wars of intervention against Iraq, Libya, and Syria—all based on lies—as well as various destabilizations and attempted color revolutions, were the result.

The battle being fought right now in the United States between this "unholy alliance" and the intelligence apparatus from the Bush/Obama period, on the one side, and a patriotic grouping of whistleblowers and Trump voters on the other, is no internal American matter; it is of the highest strategic significance. If the neocons succeed, global war against Russia and China is pre-programmed.

Building housing the MI6 headquarters in London.

historycommons.org

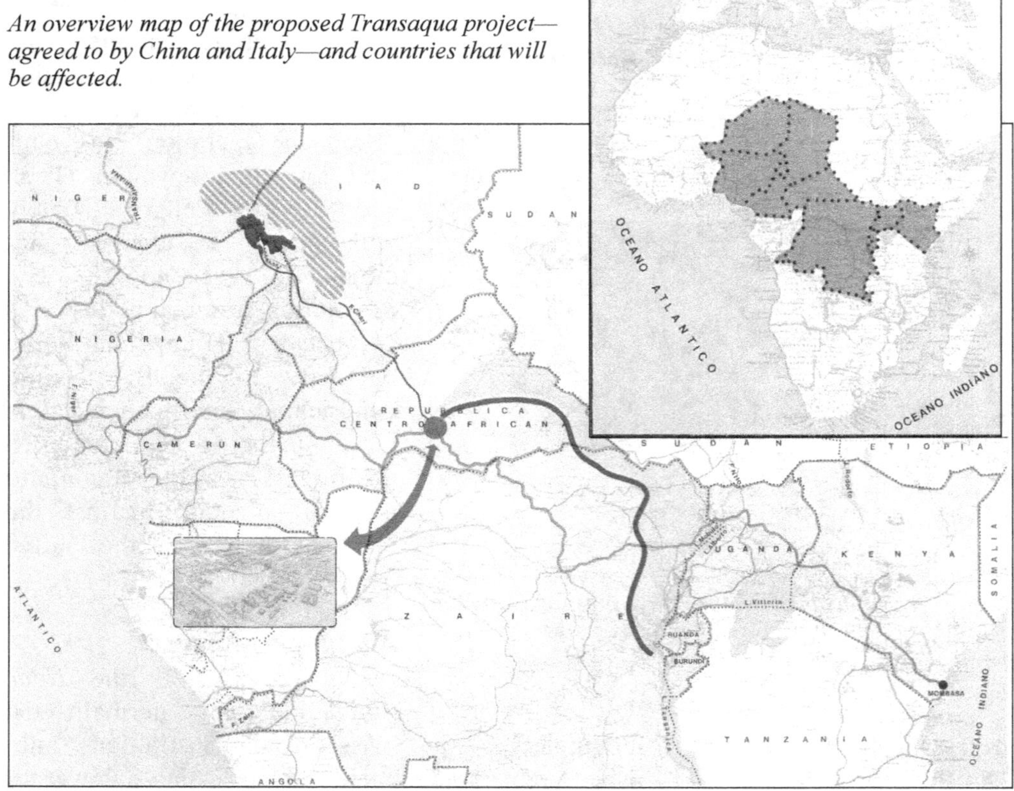

An overview map of the proposed Transaqua project—agreed to by China and Italy—and countries that will be affected.

he said that his two predecessors have spent six trillion dollars for senseless wars in the Near and Middle East, and as a result there is no money to maintain the schools. Because of these bad governments, people look to the future with despair and pessimism, even if somewhat less today than under the Obama Administration.

And what is the German population suffering from? From a government which—like the three monkeys—is deaf, blind, and dumb to the dark side of the policy of the "western community of values," from whose consequences the majority of people have suffered. It is interesting, however, that Foreign Minister Sigmar Gabriel now speaks of the "so-called West." At the time people began talking about the "so-called DDR"—the German Democratic Republic under Communist rule—its fate was already sealed.

of the extension of the New Silk Road, help overcome poverty, underdevelopment, and hopelessness. We can now actually forecast with certainty that the greatest infrastructure project ever devised for Africa, the Transaqua project, just agreed upon between China and Italy, will actually contribute to fundamentally changing the character of a large part of the African continent for the better, as well as to solving the refugee crisis in a human way. This is a project that will fill Lake Chad again and bring inland navigation, hydroelectric power, and water for agriculture to 12 African states.

What does all this have to do with the theme of this article? A great deal. The optimism of the Chinese people comes not only from the fact that they have experienced an enormous improvement in their own living standards over the last 40 years, but from a large portion of Chinese citizens being aware that China's Silk Road policy has become a force for good in the world.

Conversely, the American people has seen the downhill slide of the country ever since the murder of President Kennedy. President Trump was right when

There is a very simple way for the German people to return to optimism about their future. We must win a majority for the idea that Germany should officially cooperate with the perspective of the New Silk Road, and should—together with China, Russia, and an America freed of British imperial influence—ensure the economic development of Southwest Asia and Africa. To do that, we must learn to recognize the impact which the constant stream of propaganda through the mainstream media has had on us, to free our minds of all the media rubbish of prejudices against Trump, Putin, and China, and reflect on the wisdom of the fresco painter Ambrogio Lorenzetti.

It is up to the citizenry whether Germany will become a force for good in the world. The BüSo has the right program for that. You can vote for it on September 24.

The China Wave: The Rise of A Civilizational State

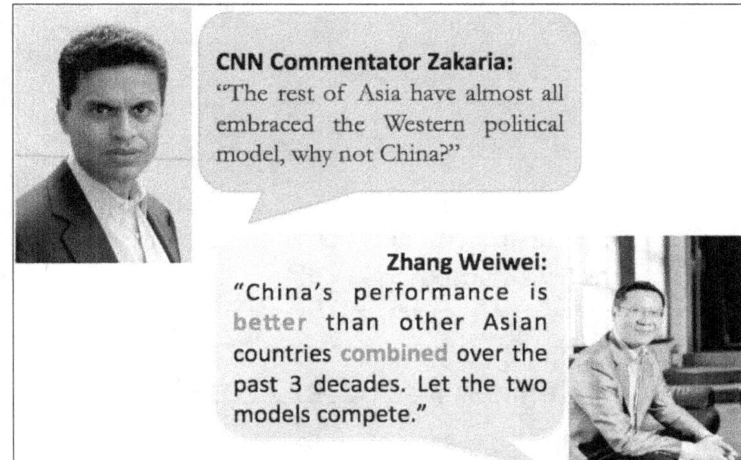

Thank you chair, and thank you, Mme. LaRouche for your kind invitation. It is a great honor to come to the Schiller Institute, to Germany, to present my views on the China model and its possible implications. I will speak for about forty-five minutes, or slightly more, and then eventually we will have questions and answers.

Let us start with an interesting encounter between myself and Fareed Zakaria, the renowned CNN host. He asked me once, at a conference: "My goodness, you always say China is unique and the Western model cannot apply to China. Well, why have all the Asian countries except China adopted the Western model?" [laughs] So, I asked the chairman of the conference how much time I had—the maximum was one minute, because it was already over time. So I said in a single statement: "Because China has performed better than all the other Asian countries combined over the past three decades. It's as simple as that." And I added, "Behind this, of course, is what I call the China model. Let's compare the China model and U.S. model and see which model works better."

This is a quick slide to show the huge reduction of poverty in China. Actually, 70% of the world's poverty eradication has occurred in China. In other words, without China's performance in wiping out poverty, poverty in the world would have actually grown, rather than been reduced.

Here are some major indices about China's rapid development: Roughly over the last three decades and a half, China has been growing at an annual rate of nine percent, trade fifteen percent, per year. China has now become the world's largest trading nation. Its total GDP, by official exchange rate figures with the U.S. dollar, is almost $11 trillion. What's more important, if you calculate this by purchasing power parity (PPP), then China is was already an economy larger than the United States three years ago; those are the IMF statistics.

Why should China follow others?

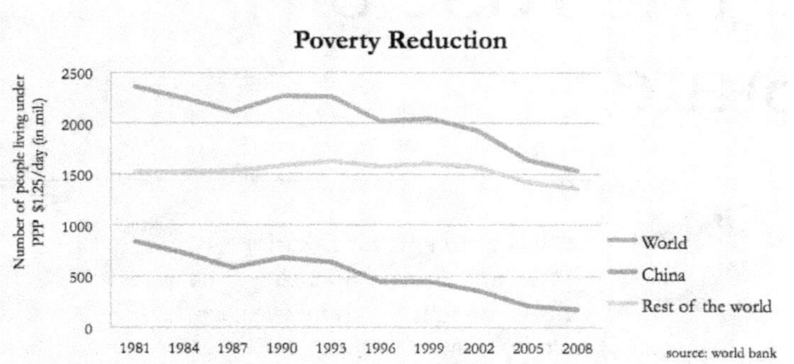

In terms of eradicating poverty and creating middle class, China has performed better than the rest of Asian countries combined

China's Rise （1979-2015）

- Annual GDP growth rate: 9 %
- Annual trade growth rate: 15%
- Total GDP: US$ 10.9 trillion (2015)
- Total GDP (ppp): US$ 17.6 trillion (2014)
- Total trade volume: US$ 4.3 trillion (2015)
- Poverty reduction: 700 million and MDG
- Foreign ex. reserves: US$ 4 trillion (2014)
- Outbound tourists: 135 million visits(2016)
- About the future: 87% optimistic (PEW 2014)

China is the largest trading nation, with a $4.3 trillion total annual trade volume, while having lifted 700 million people out of poverty. China is the first developing country to realize, to achieve the United Nations Millennium Development Goal (MDG), which means to halve poverty by the year 2010. China did that a long time ago. And China also has the world's largest foreign exchange reserves, which means that China's foreign exchange reserves alone are now larger than the combined economies of the former Socialist countries, including Russia, the Central Asian Republics, and the Eastern and Central European countries—larger than their GDP put together, the foreign exchange reserves alone.

Last year, China exported more tourists than any other country—135 million visits made abroad, which means that China has produced the world's largest middle class. This is by international law standards, which means you hold a passport and go abroad.

China's a huge country. Flying from Beijing to Shanghai, covers the equivalent of ten European countries. Virtually all those who can afford air travel in China, all those who can ride high-speed trains, are those who can afford to go abroad.

What's more important is that most Chinese are optimistic about the future of their country—this is very important—and also about the future of their own lives and their families. So this is very encouraging.

Political Reforms

Now, exactly at that time, six years ago, I had a debate with Francis Fukuyama, the author of *The End of History*. He came to Shanghai at the time of the Arab Spring, when Egyptian President Mubarak had stepped down, when the Arab Spring was sweeping across much of North Africa and the Middle East. So we debated ten issues—but three of them I will share with you. We predicted the future: One prediction concerned the Arab Spring, and he said that China may also go through an "Arab Spring," like Egypt. I said, "no chance," and I explained why, and I gave all kinds of reasons. Then I predicted accurately, that the Arab Spring would become an "Arab Winter." That was in June 2011, I checked; I may be the first scholar to have made this prediction. I was in Brussels last year; I told EU officials, "If the EU would only have listened to the views of Chinese scholars like me six years back, you could have avoided this refugee crisis."

And then, Fukuyama and I discussed political reforms in China and in the United States. He said, "Yes, there are a lot of problems in the U.S. political system, but," he said, "it's a mature political system. It can fix its own problems." I replied, "I doubt it." I said, "Your political system is a product of the pre-industrial era, when the U.S. had a population of slightly less than three million." "So," I said, "you have to go through substantial reform." I made another prediction, which was also accurate, "Without such reform, my concern is your next President may be worse off than George W. Bush." And today, I guess, most Americans may share

A government of the people, by the people, for the people...

---

this view; for sure, most Europeans will share this view given the Trump phenomenon.

And then I said, number three, "It's not the end of history, but the end of the end of history." And I explained why to him. Of course, one major reason is the rise of China, which I call a civilizational state, in that it has its own logic, different from other countries.

Now, let's discuss the China model, and let's first focus on the political dimension of the China model: democracy. How to define democracy? It's not easy. Let me borrow the famous line from Abraham Lincoln:

For the people

A comparison between US-CHINA's Net Household Assets at medium level

Resource: Survey of US's Consumer Finance 2012, by FED, the USA, and Investigation on China's Family Financial Report 2012, by Southwestern University of Finance and Economics, CHINA

"government of the people, by the people, for the people," and then compare China and the United States and maybe some other Western countries, to see in the end, who has done better, in terms of "of the people, by the people, for the people."

Let's start with "for the people" first. This is a slide to show the increase of the wealth of the Chinese people, and the decline of the wealth of American families. Look at household net assets. The gap between Chinese families and U.S. families is roughly only 10,000 U.S. dollars. It's unbelievable, but it's true. This is a Pew Center survey, which shows that most Chinese are optimistic about their country's future, and are satisfied with the direction of their country. In China, it's 87%, in the U.S.A. 37%.

And this is the latest one, by Ipsos, U.K., one of the largest opinion survey companies. They ask whether the citizens of their countries consider their countries are on the right track: in the case of China, it's 90%; in the case of United States, 35%. I don't know why in the case of Germany, it's pretty low—it's 32%! But that's Ipsos' survey; maybe by this time, half a year later, it's already different. But anyway, you see the result of this survey.

So, the above, as I said, is "for the people," where China has done arguably better than the United States.

"Of the people": If we look at civil servants, the composition of civil service officials, in the case of China, 95% of Chinese civil servants come from very ordinary families. So we see the People's Republic is made up of ordinary people; this is technically true as well for the Chinese government. For the United States, Professor Stiglitz of Columbia University, Economics Nobel Prize Laureate, famously said, "the United States today is of the one percent, by the one percent, for the

Of the People

95% of Chinese civil servants come from ordinary background.

From speech by Minister Yin Weimin, 9 Jan. 2013

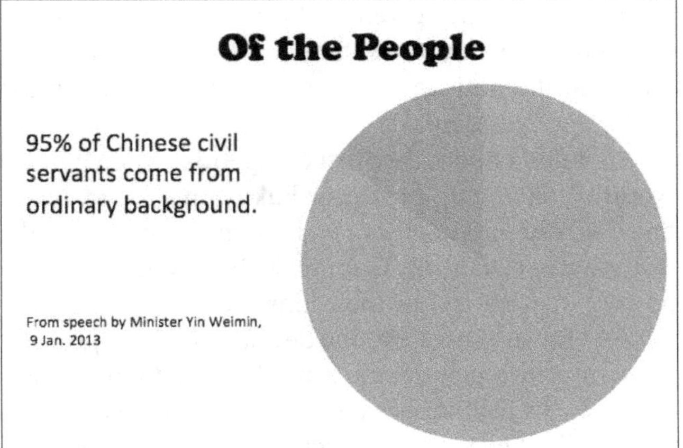

By the people ?

- If multiparty and universal suffrage mean government by people, why "elect and regret" all the time?
- Forms produce substance or substance produces forms.
- China explores substance first.
- A paradigm shift: good governance vs bad governance, not democracy vs autocracy

The making of Five-Year Plans

one percent." This line has been widely quoted in the media.

Democracy

Now, actually the dispute comes with this "by the people." So what is, really, "by the people?" In the West, in Germany as well, democracy is widely associated with very simple procedural democracy—one person, one vote, plus a multiparty system, and regular elections and rotation of governments. Yet, we find that in many countries, Western democracy is,— there is this phenomenon called, "elect and then regret." If we look at the Brexit in the U.K., if you look at the U.S. election last year, and we look at opinion surveys about the U.S. Congress, its approval rate is something around 10%.

So here there is a contrast. The Western approach of democracy is focused on what's called "procedural democracy"—procedurally that's correct, it is democracy. The Chinese approach it differently: China says, let's first look at substance. So what's the objective of democracy?—then, try to explore what are the best ways and means to achieve this end, and this is the essence of democracy. So we have conducted wide, extensive experiments—I'll come to that. I call this a paradigm shift from what's called "democracy vs autocracy," to "good governance vs bad governance." In other words, democracy at the level of substance, should be good governance.

How to achieve good governance? Each country, each nation should explore approaches, procedures appropriate to its national conditions, and that is the approach China has adopted. This is what China has tried

out, in terms of the political system. I say, if the Western approach is about elections, the Chinese approach is about selection plus elections. And selection is part of Chinese culture: We have a long tradition. China was the first country that invented the public civil service exam system, what we call *keju,* by the Sui Dynasty, which means 1,500 years ago. We call this system "meritocracy."

For the top leadership in China today, we have what's called the members of the Standing Committee of the Political Bureau. The minimum requirement is having served two terms as a governor of a Chinese province, which means, at minimum, since China is the world's most populous country, you have to have already governed 100 million people before you become one of the top seven. In the case of Xi Jinping, he actually managed three provinces, Fujian, Zhejiang and Shanghai. The internal population is 120 million. In terms of the size of the economy, it's larger than India— all before he became a member of the Standing Committee. Then he was given another five years in this particular membership, to get familiar with national affairs, affairs at the national level, and then became the top leader, the President.

So, I think this is the most competitive system in the world! I joked with Professor Fukuyama, I said, "with the Chinese meritocracy system, it's inconceivable, that a weak leader like George W. Bush could come to power." It's way below the Chinese bar.

And this is what I call the decision-making process. We term it new democratic centralism. Actually, democratic centralism originated with the Soviet Union. Eventually it became more centralism than democracy.

China's democratic experiments (3)

Consultative democracy
across the state and society (the mass line)

The Chinese State and the Party

China is a civilizational state, and the Communist
Party of China is a continuation of China's long
tradition of a unified Confucian ruling entity.

But China turned this process, really, changed it completely. It's really an institutionalized decision-making process. Essentially, it's what we call "from the people, to the people," the first round; "to the people, from the people," another round; "from the people, to the people, again." You go through several rounds of consultations and in the end you reach better decisions.

A typical example is China's Five-Year Plan. Again, it's a product from the Soviet Union, but China has moved way beyond the Soviet model. It's not mandatory planning, it's strategic-indicative planning; it's the orientation of the country, orientation of the economy, orientation of social development. For instance, China made a decision five years ago to make renewable energy a strategic sector. So now China is *the* leader in renewable energies, whether solar power, wind power, or electric cars—China is the leader in terms of investment and output.

But this same process goes through hundreds of rounds of discussions at different levels of Chinese government and society, with input from many, many think-tanks. In the end, we reach consensus. So it's very different from the American model which is decisions by a small circle who then try to sell that to the public. We don't need to sell it. This legitimacy of the decision-making process is much stronger than in the American practice.

And then we have, at the grass roots level, what we call consultative democracy, across the state and society. In the West, essentially, democracy is confined to regular elections in the political domain, about who will become the next leader. In the case of China, it's really a part of social life. For instance, in my university, my institute, we have a union which will casts votes on the performance of the director, deputy director, and secretary general. We do this once a year. You want to promote, say, middle-level cadre—we did that just last month; then you have a list of all of those who are qualified, you have opinion surveys for all of them, all the professors, associate professors, and lecturers. This is what's called the "mass line" in the official jargon.

The Chinese State

Now, what's more fundamental, is how to understand the Chinese state. I described the Chinese state as a civilizational state. What does that mean? China is unique: China is the world's longest continuous civilization. And this civilization is amalgamated with a super-large modern state. It's actually made up of hundreds of states made into one. I once said, more or less accurately: if you are familiar with China, you can observe the way of life and mentality of a typical person from Shanghai, a typical Pekinese, a typical Cantonese—three major cities in China. The differences between these three groups of people are actually wider and greater than among a typical German, Frenchman and Englishman—even to their language, their dialects, and internal pronunciation. The gap is bigger than between German and English, or French—but we have the same written language, and this is important.

So the Chinese are not just one state— like Austria—it's totally different. I will use another phrase; it's not accurate, but to have a European audience understand, it's more as if the Roman Empire had continued to this day. People speak their different dialects, but they all use Latin as a written language, and then there

Cancel the British System, Save the People   11

is a centralized government, a modern economy, and the world's largest middle class —something like that. It's not accurate but it's a useful analogy.

So this kind of state cannot afford today's Western political system; if you tried this system, the country would break up immediately. Just like the Roman Empire, if it continued today, would break up with the Western political system.

For this kind of country, the political tradition of running this kind of country, the political governance or political culture for state-governance or statecraft, *is always* a unified ruling entity, a united political entity. So the Chinese Communist Party is different from the Republican Party or Democratic Party. Those Western political parties are openly representative of certain groups, and then they compete with each other for election.

In the case of China, it is such a huge country. It was first unified in 221 B.C., 2,200 years ago. Ninety-five percent or more of the time, China was under one, unified political entity, the emperor, the court—and this situation continues to this day. So I call the Chinese Communist Party a grand coalition.

You have all kinds of different voices, interests, ways, within the party, but you have to reach consensus and move on the consensus. So sometimes, I use another term. As I said, in the West, political parties are openly representative of partial interests, the interests of certain groups: In the case of China, even with its long past, you have to represent so-called "all under Heaven." If you cannot represent, you have to claim you represent "all under Heaven." If you claim you represent only part of the society, you cannot come to power at all. This is a very different political tradition.

This is my quick summary of the so-called "China model." And politically, essentially, it's selection plus election: You have a vigorous process of selection, and then you have a process of election. And you have a unified ruling entity—today it's called the Communist Party. Many people don't like this name, especially in the West. For Germany, you have the East Germany experience, but what's more important is the substance. Some people in the West always think China is nothing but another East Germany, but ten times larger.

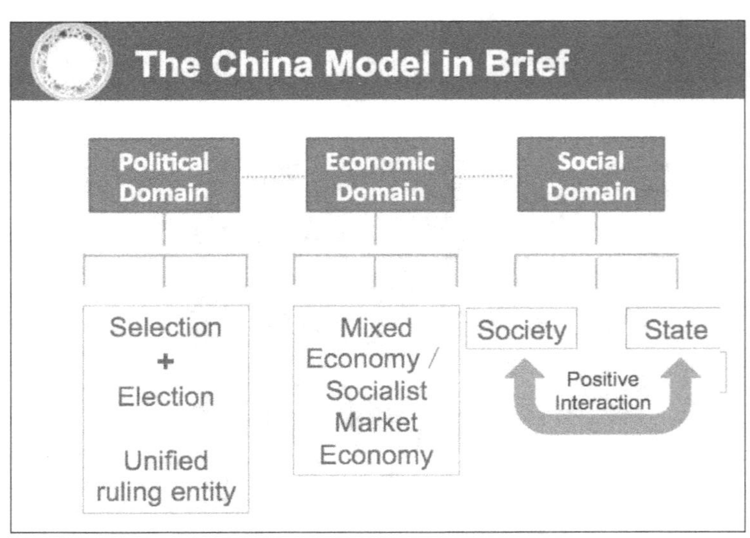

No—it's very different. It's a civilization, a civilizational state, and many traditions continue.

The Economy

In the economic domain, China is a mixed economy. It's officially called a socialist market economy. In the West, there's the difference between the continental model, in which the state plays a larger role, versus the Anglo-Saxon model. But in the case of China, you have state ownership of land. We are all property owners, but we have a contract with the state: You own the right to use this piece of land for seventy years, and then it will be renewed. The advantage of this system is China can carry out this larger-scale infrastructure development in the public interest.

And then, when I say "mixed economy," I can give an example. China is now leading the world in mobile phone technology. What's our objective? We call this, the "fourth industrial revolution"—with one mobile phone you can do everything. For instance, in Shanghai, you don't need a credit card, you don't need cash; everything is paid by your mobile phone. It's already achieved. And today this mobile phone payment in China is already larger than Japan's GDP. It's fifty times that in the United States.

And behind the mixed economy—China now has a company, you must have heard of it, called Alibaba, of Jack Ma. He invented a shopping festival, shopping spree, Double 11, so 11.11, for Singles. But actually it's for everyone. So, in the Double 11 festival last year, the one day e-commerce volume was larger than the e-

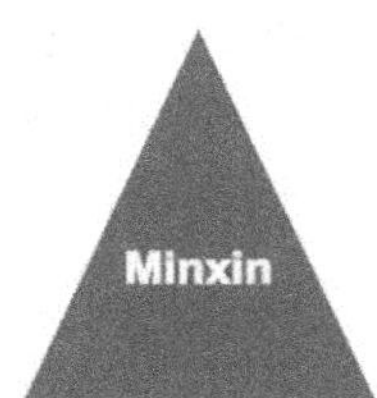

Mencius (372-289 BC)

commerce volume of the whole country of India in one year. It's 120.7 billion yuan, or about $18 billion; it's larger than India's e-commerce for the whole year. Jack Ma's Alibaba is a private company, and it's doing extremely well.

But, I say it's a mixed economy: The whole logistics, highway, expressways, high-speed trains, this mobile system—4G, 5G—now, 4G already covers the whole country, 99%, and it's a vast country, all these are done by state-owned companies. It's indeed a combination of two sectors, the state sector and the private sector. China's a vast country, and you have many villages in the mountains, but China started a project called the "Hard-Paved Ways to Each and Every Village," which has been achieved. Power, electricity coverage for the whole nation has been achieved. So all these are done by the state sector. So, indeed, this is mixture of both state sector and private sector. The private sector is extremely dynamic, and then you also have the important role of the state sector.

In the social domain, it's more about interactions between the state and society, rather than—especially as against the American model—society *versus* state, society *against* the state is different. Because, in the United States, the tradition is the state is a "necessary evil." But in the case of China, the state has long been viewed as a necessary virtue. In China's long history, two major rivers, the Yangtze River and Yellow River, run across much of the country. The two rivers cause regular floods, and we have to control the floods. To control a flood, nationwide coordination is needed; no single province can perform this job. That's why China has shaped this long tradition of a slightly larger role for the central government. So whatever surveys you do, the central government always enjoys tremendous support among the Chinese public. This is almost always the case.

Minxin and *Minyi*

Now, this is important—the philosophy behind Chinese statecraft. Today, we have this issue of "populism," and in my debate with Professor Fukuyama, I said, "I'm deeply worried about the rise of simple-minded populism in the United States." He said, with confidence, "even Abraham Lincoln famously said, 'you can fool some of the people some of the time, but not all of the people all of the time.' You know, with the free media, with freedom of speech, we can correct these mistakes." I said, "I'm not that optimistic." [laughs] I'm being slightly cynical, because I know the United States well.

In the end, indeed, populism causes a lot of problems. But in Chinese statecraft, this idea of popular opinion is called *minyi;* and then there is *minxin*—one has still to find the right translation; I have tried to use the expression "hearts and minds of the people." In other words, *minyi* is more or less public opinion; *minxin* is more about the long-term and overall interest of your nation, or your country. So the governance in China is based on *minxin,* very importantly. *Minyi,* or public opinion, could reflect *minxin,* the "hearts and minds," the long-term intentions of your country, or could not reflect it—because in the Internet age, in this new social media age, public opinion can shift in minutes or hours.

So I think at this moment of time in history, emphasis on *minxin* is crucially important. Fortunately we have a system which can do that, through what we call "consultative democracy."

And this is interesting. I just tried to show you a study done by an American scholar: that in the West we hear very often, even in Germany, of so-called "European values," or "universal values." This term itself is okay. The point is, to what extent is it really universal? This study was actually the product of the debate about "Asian values" in the 1990s. They suggest that, yes, there are certain values which all peo-

Priority of values: East Asia vs. USA

(D. Hutchcock's survey, 1994)

	East Asia	USA
• 1.	Social order	Freedom of Speech
• 2.	Harmony	Individual rights
• 3.	Acountability	Individual freedom
• 4.	Open to new ideas	Public debate

Reflections on American democracy

Three genetic flaws?
- Rational human being assumption.
- Absolute rights.
- Procedures all that important.

Three institutional weaknesses:
- Democracy or mone-talkracy?
- Weak governance (e.g. Fukuyama: Vetocracy)
- Indebted economy

ples of all nations share. Yet, due to different political and cultural traditions, these values are given different priorities. In the United States, it's freedom of speech; in East Asia—there is almost no exception—it's public order. And the reason is very simple, because you have a very large population and you have relatively smaller, per-capita resources. So if there is no social order, it's chaos. If you ask a Chinese, what do you fear most, he will tell you "chaos." So this is the key difference.

But, always, I share this view with my American friends: I say, do you really have freedom of speech? The United States is such a "politically correct" society! You have so many taboos, far more taboos than China, that you cannot touch upon. But that's the same with the European countries—even in Germany, as well, you have this problem.

That's my thinking about the American model. In my debate with Fukuyama, I mentioned briefly the problem with the U.S. system, why it's not the end of history; it's the end of the end of history, because there are certain things, which are like genetic flaws—one is this assumption that human beings are rational, and this whole idea of one person, one vote based on that! Indeed, with the new social media, you find that increasingly it's difficult to keep rational and reasoned discussions. In the United States, with the involvement *of the money,* and then the new social media, you want to be rational? It's not that easy.

And then, rights have become absolute. That's in Europe as well. Rights, rights, rights! From a humble Chinese view, rights and obligations always go together, otherwise the society cannot operate on a long-term basis.

The Belt and Road

And then, the procedures are always the most important thing. I agree, procedures *are* very important, but look at the West today, the United States in particular. From my humble observation of the world today, all countries need some kind of reforms, the United States, Germany, European countries, Chinese Taiwan, Hong Kong they all need reforms! *But!*—Actually, most countries can hardly conduct reform. For one thing, the procedures are so complicated. For instance, if you want to have reform in the United States, you need to revise the Constitution. Actually, it's impossible to revise the Constitution. As a result you cannot carry out reforms.

China is arguably one of the very few countries which can push reforms. Now in the United States, the problem is democracy or money-talkracy. I think, in the year 2010 and the year 2014, the Supreme Court of the United States decided not to set a ceiling for campaign contributions for companies or individuals. You can contribute as much as you want. So this is not a democracy, it's a "money-talkracy," i.e., the key message is "money talks."

And then, the issue of weak governance—Fukuyama's phrase called it a "vetocracy," different institutions veto each other; then the economy is heavily in debt.

Now, this will be an interesting fallout from the China model. I will describe the China model, and how it operates, and then its relation with the Belt and Road Initiative. So I will describe how the model operates in terms of ideas, in terms of the model's features, and then see their relations with the Belt and Road Initiative.

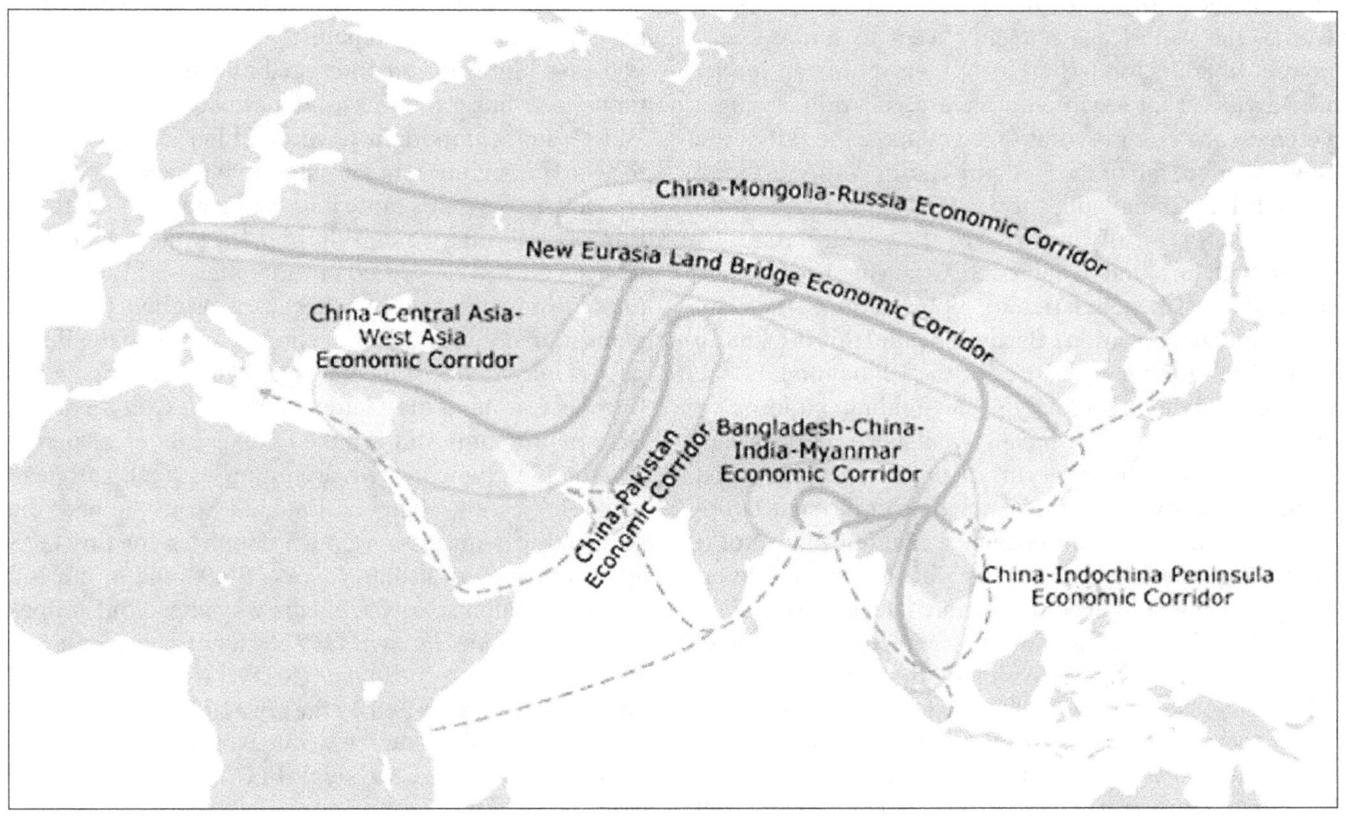

You know that the Chinese President put forward this Belt and Road Initiative four years ago. It's really about a platform across Eurasia on land and sea routes from China through the South China Sea all the way to the Indian Ocean, South Asia, Africa, Europe, and to Indonesia.

So this is a gigantic project, and when it was first put forward four years ago, and even now, it always meets a lot of suspicion in the West. If you look at the Western doubts, or suspicions, they are mainly twofold: One is, China is now an economy with excessive industrial capacity; it wants to export this excessive industrial capacity. This is one interpretation.

The other is geopolitical: China has geopolitical intentions, to create this new sphere of influence. And in honesty, I must say, yes, China has indeed excessive industrial capacity, so this argument stands. China wants to export its excessive capacity. And given the size of this project—it will cover 4.4 billion people along the routes—of course it will have geopolitical and geo-economic fallout. No doubt about this.

But, I think if you only confine yourself to these two considerations, you miss a lot of far more important implications of this initiative. The China model has one feature better than the Western model, which is, *it can plan for the future*. It really plans for the next and next-after-that generations, for the next fifty to one hundred years. I will explain how the China model operates in this whole initiative.

First, this is called, "people's livelihood first." We all know, at this moment of history, a lot of countries—European countries included—are experiencing a de-globalization. People are not happy with globalization. China is one of the very few countries that has, indeed, benefitted from globalization. You may say that China is the largest beneficiary from globalization. Why so? What's the Chinese secret?

Actually, it's very simple: Because China defines globalization *only* as economic globalization, not as political globalization—that's the key difference. Because, over the past twenty or so years, globalization was actually what's called "neoliberal globalization."

It's about privatization; that's already political. It's about democratization—that's very political. In other words, the Americans not only want to impose economic liberalization, but also their political model worldwide. That's why you have this "Arab Spring," you have the color revolutions, you have the fall of the Soviet Union, fall of the East, the Berlin Wall, etc. Good or bad, but China said, "for us, globalization is only economic. Politically, no." That's the key difference.

So with this kind of approach, China has become one of the largest beneficiaries of globalization. And why economic globalization? Because behind this is Chinese logic, one of the key features of the China model: "the people's livelihood first," is the guiding philosophy. What does it mean? It means whatever you do—economic reform, social reform, or political reform—you should not allow the political machine or the state structure to operate in vain or become a chatting shop. No! It has to do something concrete, tangible for people's lives. It could be material; it could be more than material, but it has to boil down to something concrete, for the people. And thus, "The people's livelihood first." It reminds me of the famous line from Bill Clinton, when he said, "It's the economy, stupid." He advised those politicians who wanted to become prime minister or President, "Pay attention to economic performance." So China has all along focused on this, trying to improve people's living standards, rather than chanting empty slogans.

The second part, again, of the China model's philosophy, is "seeking truth from facts." That's the famous line from Deng Xiaoping, China's late leader. He said, we should seek truth from facts, not from dogmas, whether it's from communist dogma or from capitalist dogma; whether it's East dogma or West dogma. East dogma is a utopian outlook; Western dogma is about democracy—the markets represent the best, and the rest is nonsense. So Deng said we should try our own approach, because it's Chinese-style socialism. In the end, it has worked.

Then you have this "opening up at home and abroad." In the Belt and Road Initiative, it becomes what we call "connectivity." Connectivity at the policy level, at the infrastructure level, in the trade level, at customs levels.

True Economic Development

And I will try to introduce another concept: It's called "vertical connectivity." I mentioned "horizontal connectivity," especially infrastructural links between nations. At the vertical level it's also interesting: You have the underground pipelines for oil, for natural gas; you have highway construction, bullet trains, or normal trains, sea links, air links—it's already a bit vertical. What's more important now, is China is also putting forward cooperation in the satellite business.

And then, what's more interesting has to do with the Europeans, what we call the *Beidou* system, which is China's GPS system. And unfortunately, the Europeans missed an opportunity, because originally, China planned to do this project in cooperation with the European Union. We signed a strategic agreement: for Europe you have the Galileo program; China has the Beidou program. And yet, the EU has a lot of suspicion about China, whether we are going to steal European technologies, or whatever. [laughs] So in the end, the partnership with the European countries for this GPS system broke up; it didn't work. So, China in the end has done it alone. Now, China is way ahead of Europe.

So China has its own GPS system for the Belt and Road countries; by next year, 2018, it will cover all Belt and Road countries, and by the year 2020, in three years from now, it will cover the whole world; so it will be an alternative to the GPS system. In China we use this already.

So this is what I called "vertical connectivity."

Then, "consultative democracy." I mentioned this already briefly. In the Belt and Road Initiative, the slogan and methodology is called "discussing together or planning together, building together, and benefitting together." In other words, a country, out of its own interest, decides to join this initiative, or not; China will not impose its view on you. If you feel it's in your interest, you can join. If it's not in your interest, you don't need to join; it's voluntary. So this is in part a fallout from the China model, what we call "consultative democracy."

And then, more important, in the China model we have a relatively strong state, but I mentioned the historical legacies from China's long history as a civilizational state. It's also relatively neutral, and relatively disinterested. In the Chinese model, the central government plays a central role, because you have the different regions in China, and they also have their own interests. The central government must remain relatively neutral so that they can take care of overall interests.

How the China Model operates and the B&R

- People's livelihood first
- Seeking truth from facts
- Opening up at home and abroad
- Consultative democracy
- A unified, neutral and pro-development state
- Sense of priorities and sequences
- Compass, rather than road maps
- Building bridges between the old and the new
- Creating new drivers for growth
- Shaping an irresistible trend & reshaping globalization

I'll mention again, China is not a small country. I made a rough calculation: in Europe each country is roughly 14 million people on average, per nation, per county. China is 1.4 billion people. So China is one hundred times the size of the average European state. As a result, when we look at globalization up to now, what many countries, especially developing countries are concerned with about the existing international institutions—with the IMF/World Bank, WTO, you name it—they are, from a non-Western countries' point of view, biased toward the West, rather than toward the developing countries. As a result, China said, let's do something more neutral—and we tried the AIIB, the Asian Infrastructure Investment Bank, and the Silk Road Fund, etc. So these are ideas which originated from China, backed with Chinese money and other money. This is important.

And they also have a "sense of priorities and sequences." If you look at China as a whole, the whole reform process started with the countryside, with agriculture, and then industry, and then commerce. It started with the coastal areas, and then the interior parts of China. The same with the Belt and Road Initiative: We have the idea of what we call the "key projects," or "pivot projects," and "pivot countries." It's not all the countries simultaneously. You have conditions that differ from one to another. Some countries have more mature conditions, so we do it first—and then try to have what we call the demonstration effect, to show others, so others can decide to follow or not. So there is a "sense of priorities and sequences."

Another interesting phenomenon—many Europeans asked, "Can it be successful?" We met some scholars yesterday, who said, "You do not have a road map." Europeans believe that you must have clear guidelines, a clear road map, and clear rules to go by, and then we can do it. Otherwise, we have suspicions, reservations. But the Chinese approach, if you look at the four decades of change since 1978, is different. We start "not with a road map, we start with a compass." We just know the orientation, the direction. And Deng Xiaoping said, the orientations are clear: first, improving people's living standards, and second, a more market-oriented economy. So, market orientation, and people's livelihood, are the two orientations.

And under this orientation, you encourage all kinds of experiments, and the central government will say, "this experiment is great, let's do it, extend it nationwide. That experiment is not successful, we should stop it." So that's the overall approach. Most probably a road map will emerge in due course. Not now, perhaps ten years from now for the Belt and Road Initiative. So now there are some interesting developments all the time.

And then, "building bridges between the old and the new." This is also a very important feature of how the China model operates. For instance, in the process of China's change over the past four decades, the reforms of the state sector came much later; we have kept the state sector intact, but we created a private sector from scratch, and then we tried to build a bridge between the state sector and the private sector, and let them compete with each other. And the state sector *has* to reform itself, and then become partners. That's the overall approach.

So in the Belt and Road Initiative, the same thing is happening. You have the existing arrangement—like in Russia, they have what's called the Eurasian Economic Union. China said, "You stay with that, and we'll build a bridge between the BRI and your plan." Same with Kazakhstan: They have what's called a Shining Road and we said, "Stay with that, and we'll build a bridge between the two," so the two sides can cooperate.

And then, we have the great new economy, new drivers. So the Chinese model has this: If you ask a Chinese official how to develop an economy, he will

Chinese Socialism: Success and its future

1. the world's largest economy now or soon (one UK every three years)
2. a middle class twice the US population in a decade (world's largest "propertied class")
3. medical insurance and pension for all.
4. the largest number of outbound tourists.
5. the world leader in alternative energies.
6. paradigm shift: good or bad governance vs. democracy or autocracy
7. global impact: vertical to horizontal order.

study with you what will be the possible new drivers for the economy. Then, let's do it together, developing the new drivers. Last year, in Hangzhou, we hosted the G-20 summit. Why the choice of Hangzhou? Because Hangzhou is the headquarters of Alibaba and other large companies—extremely dynamic. It's the first Chinese city in which you can survive without cash, without credit cards. You can buy a bottle of water with your mobile phone—it's very easy. So the new economy shows the road.

The Road Ahead

There's a Chinese word, called *shi,* which means overall trend. In playing the Chinese game of "go," it's somewhat like chess, but different from chess. The purpose is not to physically destroy one enemy, or two enemies. It's to create space and trends. If these trends are favorable to you, others will follow and there will be no other choices. It's like the AIIB, the Asian Infrastructure Investment Bank. The United States said, "No, it's not good." Japan said, "No." But China created a trend, *shi,* so all the other countries wanted to join, and the U.K. took the lead! Germany is also part of it. By the end of this year, we expect the AIIB will have a membership of eighty-eight or ninety members, so it will be an international financial institution already. That will really reshape globalization from what's been called a "zero-sum game" to a "win-win partnership."

And my last slide is a projection about China's future, or Chinese socialism. China will become the world's largest economy in ten years—that's by official exchange rates. If it's by purchasing power parity, China is already the largest economy. And China now produces the size of one U.K. economy, with its extra GDP, created every three years.

And China's middle class will be twice the U.S. population in a decade. Today, China's middle class is about 300 million. So ten years from now, China will have a middle class, by my estimate, of at least 600 million, or twice the U.S. population. For one thing, China has now already produced the world's largest—I don't like the word—"propertied class." All people have properties. In the cities it's 85%, and in the countryside it's one hundred percent. And I just checked the latest data: The average room surface size is forty square meters, which is slightly larger than in Germany. It's unbelievable; it just took four decades. In Shanghai, when I was a boy, the average space for an individual was four square meters, now it's ten times bigger. It's unbelievable.

Of course, medical insurance for all, and pensions for all: China achieved that. When you look at the U.S. medical care reform, it has almost lasted for one hundred years, and is not achieved, but China has done this within five years.

And of course, the level of protection differs from region to region, but basic insurance, and pensions for all has been achieved. Also China will produce more tourists, as is the case now and in the future. And China now is the world leader in alternative energies, renewable energies.

So eventually it will have this kind of impact—we are to witness a paradigm shift from democracy versus dictatorship, to good governance or bad governance—and good governance can take the form of the Western political systems, but it also can take the form of the non-Western political systems. Likewise, bad governance can take the form of Western political systems, and can take the form of non-Western political systems.

And the global impact will be enormous. I think we have a vertical order today, in which the West, especially the United States, is above the rest, in terms of wealth, in terms of ideas. But this order will become more horizontal. So the rest, especially China, will be on a par with the West in terms of both wealth and ideas. The world will thus be indeed very different.

And many thanks! Thank you very much.

Moving the World in a Completely Different Direction

The following is an edited transcript of remarks made by founder of the Schiller Institutes Helga Zepp-LaRouche, following the presentation given by Prof. Zhang Weiwei, at the July 11 Schiller Institute event in Berlin.

I am very happy about your presentation because it was very transparent and very clear, and I think it's very important for people to understand China better, because the mainstream media has not been very objective, and I thank you very much, because this is very important.

I briefly want to say that we have a completely changed strategic situation, which most people in Germany are not entirely aware of, since the mass media here tend to be still very much wedded to the old paradigm. The new paradigm is quickly coming into being, which is influenced by the Belt and Road Initiative (BRI) in ways which are not immediately recognizable, but this is a long-term wave which has changed the world, especially in the last four years. This dynamic is the dominant factor influencing developments below the surface. Now, this changed strategic situation has very deep implications for Germany, even if Germans are not yet aware of it. I am predicting they will be aware of it very soon.

Let me just situate this in the context of the July 7-8 G-20 meeting in Hamburg, Germany, where two events had positive implications. Everybody is aware of the fact that the demonstrations and riots that took place in the streets in Hamburg, were horrible, but two excellent developments emerged from the summit. One development was the historic meeting between President Trump and President Putin. This potentially represents a complete breakthrough. It opens the possibility for a new detente, and the reason it is a big success is that the neo-liberal establishment of the trans-Atlantic sector has tried to prevent this in the last six months with the so-called Russia-gate affair.

Kremlin.ru

Russia President Vladimir Putin and President Donald Trump met at the G-20 summit in Hamburg, Germany, July 7, 2017.

In my view, this anti-Russia attack had only one aim—namely, to prevent President Trump from fulfilling his promise to improve relations with Russia once he was elected President. The accusation that he may have been given the election as a result of Russian collusion, was designed to prevent him from realizing the improvement of relations he wanted. Therefore, in a certain sense, I think the two Presidents, Putin and Trump, outfoxed their opposition and, according to Tillerson, the Secretary of State, the chemistry between them functioned well. Russian Foreign Minister Lavrov

CasonVids/youtube

President Trump and President Xi Jinping at their April 6, 2017 meeting at Mar-a-Lago.

said it was very constructive, and some of the agreements made, including the cease-fire for Syria, are holding. They also discussed Ukraine, North Korea, terrorism, and cyber problems.

I think if the two Presidents of the two largest nuclear powers are able to discuss these conflicts, it is extremely important for world peace, and everybody should be very happy about it.

Just before the G-20, President Xi was in Moscow for a meeting that Russia and China have characterized as the most important event for their respective countries this year. They deepened their friendship, they deepened the strategic partnership, they made many agreements, and they both characterized the China-Russia relationship as the best in the history of the two countries. This is very important, because on April 1, President Xi Jinping was in Florida, meeting with President Trump at Mar-a-Lago.

The two Presidents hit it off well in this meeting also; the chemistry functioned well, and there were many meetings following it. President Trump sent a high-level delegation to the Belt and Road Forum in May, led by Matt Pottinger, and Trump and Xi also met again in the context of the G-20 meeting. So the United States and China established four high-level dialogues at Mar-a-Lago—economic, political, social, and security—and at that time President Trump said that the United States intended to collaborate with the BRI.

This is very, very significant because, if you have the Presidents of the three largest and most important nations of the world, Trump, Xi Jinping, and Putin, finding bilateral communication channels, then by implication, the three are in a new strategic relationship. This is a gigantic step in the direction of the new paradigm of international relations, because if Russia, China, and the United States can work together strategically, we have made a major step in the direction of what President Xi always calls "a shared future of humanity." This is very important, because what people have not yet realized is that the Belt and Road Initiative is not just about infrastructure—economic deals—but it is about a new paradigm in which geopolitics is overcome. Geopolitics played a major role in organizing the two world wars in the last century. In an era in which thermonuclear weapons exist, if we do not overcome geopolitics, we are at risk of facing annihilation as a species.

So these two meetings are very important develop-

President Xi Jinping and President Putin signing a joint statement of the People's Republic of China and the Russian Federation on July 4, in Moscow.

ments, because a new paradigm means that you start with the interest of humanity first, and the national interest second. With this approach, it will never again be possible for the interests of one nation or a group of nations to be set against another group of nations, because you start with what is in the common interest of humanity. We can talk about this more, and what that means, in the discussion, but I think it is a concept—it is a step into a new era of mankind. It is something which has not happened before, and we will only make it as a species if we are successful in making this transition.

Of course, the U.S. mainstream media, the Democrats, and the neocons in the Republican Party, reacted to the successful Putin-Trump meeting with complete hysteria. However, Mikhail Gorbachov, the last leader of the Soviet Union, commented that this reminded him of the first meeting he had with President Reagan at the time of the end of the Soviet Union. He recalled that immediately after the successful Gorbachov-Reagan meeting, a U.S. warship entered Russian waters, and Gorbachov said: "I understood immediately this was a provocation, and that some people in the Pentagon did not want that dialogue." Gorbachov warned that this type of sabotage could happen today. And indeed it is happening.

The Transformation of Africa

The second important development at the G-20 meeting that makes me very happy, is that there are clear signs that Germany is reluctantly overcoming its hesitancy to work with China in the development of Africa. Ironically, this change came because of the election of Trump. Previously, the German position was identical with that of the European Union: "No, we don't want China to develop railroads in the Balkans, we have to have the European standard, and we determine the rules." This hampered real development to a very large extent. Then Trump was elected, and Germany said we have to unite with China as the defenders of free trade and fair trade. As a result, Germany is now looking more towards China.

Obviously, this is a very important development, because the Belt and Road Initiative is already the most powerful dynamic on the planet. If you read the *Frankfurter Allgemeine Zeitung* or *Bild Zeitung,* you may not know it, because they don't report it, but the May 14-15 Belt and Road Forum in Beijing concretized the BRI and made it the functioning basis of a new world economic system—110 nations participated. This was an historic event.

Professor Zhang and myself had the good fortune to be part of it, and I must say, this event, where you had 29 state leaders speaking, starting with a fantastic speech by President Xi Jinping—which I advise all of you to listen to [full text or video] if you haven't done so already—followed by Putin and many other world leaders. People I spoke with had a similar perception to what I had—that we were participating in the formation of a new phase of history, in which conflict is put aside, and win-win cooperation is featured instead—and this dynamic is gigantic.

There are already six major economic corridors being built. It reaches into Latin America, many different kinds of international organizations are integrating their efforts, including the Belt and Road Initiative, the Eurasian Economic Union, the Association of Southeast Asian Nations (ASEAN), and the "16 Plus One" organization of Central and East European states. In addition, countries like Italy, Portugal, Spain, and France want to cooperate—even Switzerland and Austria. It has a dynamic that is already overwhelming, and what China has done in Africa is absolutely breathtaking.

China has already built major rail lines in Africa, including from Djibouti to Addis Ababa, Ethiopia, from the port city of Mombasa to the capital Nairobi, in Kenya, and has signed a contract to build a railroad from Tanzania to central Africa, which will eventually go up to Rwanda and other inland countries.

China is building railways in Nigeria; it is now looking, together with Italy, at the largest infrastructure

Xinhua/Sun Ruibo

A passenger train on Chinese financed and built light rail in Addis Ababa, Ethiopia.

project ever, the Transaqua Project, which will bring water from the tributaries of the Congo River, at an elevation of five hundred meters, and by gravity this water will be channeled all the way to Lake Chad to refill the lake, which has dried up to only ten percent of its previous area. Once this project is finished, it will provide irrigation to twelve participating nations; it will give them inland navigation; and it will completely transform the African continent.

China has already created 300,000 jobs for Africans. It employs a 90% African workforce in all projects it is undertaking in Africa, contrary to the Western propaganda, which claims that Chinese projects only employ Chinese people. It's involved in major training programs, including dams, hydropower and agriculture projects, and industrial parks. China has already built ten industrial parks in African countries. This has led to a completely changed situation; Africans are now very self-confident, and they say that they no longer want to hear Sunday sermons by Europeans on good governance, and then have no investment. They want to have investment on an equal level; they want to be treated as business partners and not as beggars.

That changed attitude of the Africans, I think, helped to change the view of German institutions, to see that if Germany does not join China in Africa, they will be on the sidelines of history. Another very strong incentive is the new eruption of the refugee crisis, where, according to Professor Giulio Sapelli, last week, in three days alone, 50,000 people arrived in Italy from Libya. When

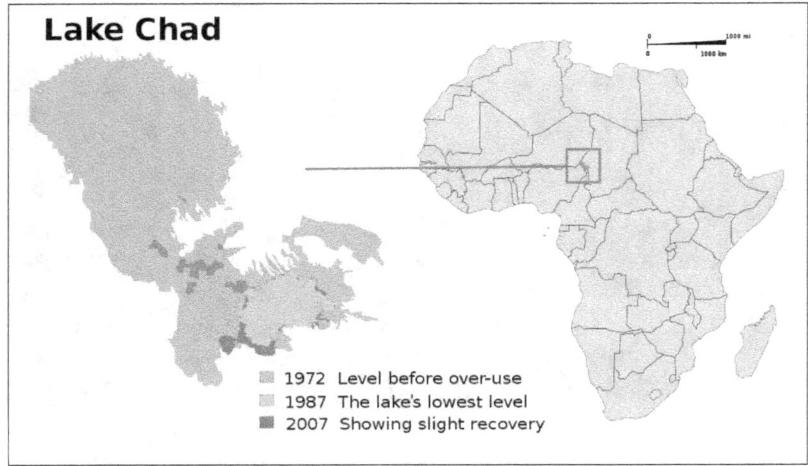

Italy requested the support of Spain and France and the other Mediterranean countries to take some of these refugee boats, they refused, so the same refugee crisis in the European Union has erupted again.

I think that these BRI-centered policy changes represent a completely changed dynamic. Remember that the financial institutions including the AIIB, the New Development Bank of the BRICS, the New Silk Road Fund, the Maritime Silk Road Fund, and the Shanghai Cooperation Bank were all created because there was almost no financing of infrastructure in the past decades. The IMF did not provide credits, the World Bank very minimally, and with bad conditions. Now a completely different financial system has emerged, which is indeed following the same principle—as Professor Zhang described as the system in China—namely, to intend to overcome poverty, and to increase living standards. If a country has the choice of either joining a military alliance and becoming an aircraft carrier in the South China Sea for the United States, or on the other hand, joining win-win cooperation with China and have economic development itself, it's obvious which is the most attractive model—and this is actually a dynamic which is already much further along than people here realize.

Trump Is Not What the Media Say

Now, as for all the people who are anti-Trump and have been convinced that he is the most evil man— well, I agree with President Putin, who after his first encounter with Trump, said that Trump is very different from the way the media portray him. That is what I have heard from many other people who have actually spoken personally with President Trump. He is not what the western media portray him as, because what he said is that he wants to stop intervention wars, he does not want to have any more foreign interventions disguised as imposing human rights and democracy. Instead he says "America First," and he said he wants to return the United States to the American System of economy, to Alexander Hamilton, to Henry Clay, to Henry C. Carey, and to Lincoln.

I have made the point repeatedly that the China model is much closer to the original American System of economy than people think. All the banking systems of China are really much more like Hamiltonian banking, or you can also say, like the policy framework of Friedrich List, the German economist, who, by the way, is the most famous economist in China today.

I think that the possibility of moving the world in a completely different direction has never been as possible as now. And the reason that I'm optimistic about Germany—and I am known to be a critic of German politics, very much so—I don't say it lightly, but the fact that Mrs. Merkel and President Xi Jinping agreed that there will be German-Chinese cooperation to build a hydroelectric complex in Angola together, and that they both said that this will be the model for future German-Chinese cooperation in the development of Africa, makes me very optimistic.

Secondly, I think that the agreement between Putin and Trump to have a cease-fire in Syria, opens up the possibility of accomplishing peace after the military intervention of Russia into Syria almost two years ago, and also opens up the possibility not only to develop Africa, but also to reconstruct the entire Southwest Asia region, from Afghanistan to Iraq to Syria to Yemen into northern Africa, a region which has been destroyed by wars that were based on lies and which have destroyed the lives of millions of people—and have, after all, caused the refugee crisis. So this new agreement between Trump and Putin, and the possibility of reconstructing the entire Near East, Southwest Asia, and Africa, will lead to the elimination of the refugee crisis. Once people have the possibility of a livelihood in their home country, they would much rather stay in their homeland. Therefore Germany should join hands not only for the development of Africa, but also for the Middle East, and then we will have a very positive future ahead of us.

Bill Browder Behind the Scenes

by Barbara Boyd

Aug. 13—Last Wednesday night (Aug. 9), this writer watched a blacklisted film, *The Magnitsky Act Behind the Scenes,* by Russian filmmaker Andrei Nekrasov. You can't see this film, because Bill Browder and his "team" have launched a worldwide campaign of threats and lawsuits, which have prevented any distributor from picking it up and showing it.

The last public showing, at the Newseum in Washington, D.C., in June 2016, resulted in a complaint to the U.S. Department of Justice, claiming everyone involved violated the Foreign Agents Registration Act (FARA).

It also resulted in a hearing before the Senate Judiciary Committee on July 27, 2017, based on Browder's FARA complaint, in which Browder was once again allowed—without challenge—to portray himself as a world-class superman of human rights and Vladimir Putin's No. 1 enemy. Browder claims the film is defamatory Russian propaganda.

After watching the film, the reason it is banned couldn't have been clearer. It demolishes Bill Browder's credibility, along with the credibility of most members of the U.S. Congress and European parliamentary bodies who have bought Browder's British intelligence-contrived tale, lock, stock, and barrel. Our Senators and Representatives have lapped up Browder's version of his alleged beef with Vladimir Putin as if they are children entranced in a simple cartoon in which Putin represents some monstrous all-consuming evil, and Bill Browder represents all that is good.

Or, as Glenn Greenwald put it 2015:

It is 100% permissible—bordering on obligatory—to spout the most insane, evidence-free

CC/Hudson Institute

William Browder

conspiracy theories if they involve Russia and Putin.

Like the sanctions in retaliation for what has now been shown to be the non-existent hacking of the computers of the Democratic National Committee, the film raises the very distinct probability that Congress is dictating foreign policy based on another completely fabricated British intelligence hoax, the Magnitsky story, as told by Bill Browder.

The infantile, brain-dead congressional fantasy-state rampant in the Senate Judiciary Committee hearing featuring Browder on July 27, fed into the anti-Russia frenzy which led to the new sanctions against Russia, which was passed by Congress on that same day, and signed under protest by President Trump on Aug. 2, 2017. These sanctions strongly enhance the hand of

EIRNS/Rachel Douglas

Street vendors and desperate bargain hunters in St. Petersburg, Russia, in 1999, as they deal with the immiseration imposed by economic shock therapy.

those who would lead us into World War III.

The Magnitsky Act sanctions against Russia were passed by Congress and signed into law by President Obama in 2012, in what then was an unprecedented punishment of Russian citizens involved in judicial matters *internal to the Russian state*. They were based solely on a story—a narrative—propounded by Browder and his public-relations crew in Washington, D.C., including Jonathan Winer of the intelligence community-connected APCO, and Juleanna Glover, press secretary to Dick Cheney, who was also a key aide to candidate John McCain, as well as being a PR partner of former Attorney General Ashcroft. Under the

Magnitsky Act, persons deemed human-rights violators by Browder and his friends can't travel to the United States or use financial institutions operating outside Russia. Putin responded by banning adoption of Russian orphans by U.S. citizens.

According to Browder's bogus narrative, he was an honest businessman in Russia, dedicated to establishing clean capitalism, and he got on the wrong side of Putin when Putin made a deal with the oligarchs controlling the finances of the Russian state, to split half their receipts with Putin, making the allegedly venal Putin the richest man in the world. Thereafter, Browder was banned from Russia as a security threat in 2005, and his companies were raided in 2007 by what he called evil thugs in the Interior Ministry, who proceeded to steal the corporate seals and articles of his companies (which at that point had no assets since Browder had spirited the money out of the country). These seals and corporate papers were then employed in a criminal scheme which robbed $230 million in fraudulent tax refunds from the Russian Treasury.

The Russian state, not Browder, was the victim of this crime. Right then, in 2007, according to Browder, he hired the "smartest lawyer" he knew, Sergei Magnitsky, who reported the tax fraud to the Russian state. The Russians had the very same Interior Ministry officials engaged in the fraud against the Russian Treasury investigate that fraud, assisted by Putin's FSB. They arrested Magnitsky, and, according to Browder, tortured him to give up his criminal complaint against them, and ultimately had him beaten to death by eight guards in a Russian prison. Then, Browder falsely claimed that they convicted the dead man, Magnitsky (see below), along with Browder, for tax fraud in 2013.

Last week in *EIR*, we established that Browder was and is a deep-penetration agent operating on behalf of the British financial interests which looted and destroyed Russia in the 1990s. Their hope was that they would have so completely decimated Russia by funding criminal gangs, oligarchs, and drugs, that they could take over the shattered country wholesale.

Putin stopped that, earning their eternal hatred. The Russians have portrayed Browder on Russian state television as a high-ranking agent of Britain's MI6, first engaged in destroying Russia under Yeltsin and now engaged in regime change operations against Putin. The *Jerusalem Post* has also called Browder an intelligence analyst for MI6.

The filmmaker, Andrei Nekrasov, a well-known Putin critic, originally set out to tell Browder's story, as told repeatedly by Browder—to Congress, to various parliamentary bodies, to corporate conferences, and on college campuses throughout the world. The first portion of the film repeats the story in all its very graphic and stereotypical anti-Russian detail, inclusive of the accused Russian mobster-ministers wearing open silk shirts and pawing loose women in drunken smoke-filled bar scenes, as they plot their nefarious crimes.

But, Nekrasov began to discover that big elements of Browder's tale don't add up. Key participants in the plot end up dead. In an interview conducted in Browder's London offices, Magnitsky's mother tells Nekrasov that she does not believe that Magnitsky was beaten to death, but rather claims he died of a heart attack and horrible medical neglect. Pavel Karpov, the central Interior Ministry villain in Browder's tale, sued Browder for libel in London. Why would Karpov do that if he were a Russian fraudster, knowing that any defamation suit opens the plaintiff to total investigation? Not only that, but, stunningly, the London Court refused to back Browder's factual claims.

The High Court of London, in the form of Mr. Justice Simon, stated that Browder, et al., had not come close to proving that Karpov was involved in the "torture" and "death" of Magnitsky or would "continue to commit, or be party to, covering up crimes." Simon tossed Karpov's suit for lack of injury in Britain, and stated that he had "set the record straight." Karpov appears for an interview with the filmmaker and convincingly gives his side of the story.

Nekrasov finds Magnitsky's statements to the police, and determines that they have been completely mistranslated on Browder's website. Magnitsky never actually made the criminal complaints about Pavel Karpov and Artem Kuznetsov which are at the very center of Browder's story. If Magnitsky was not accusing the officials of the crime, then the whole whistle-blower-retaliation narrative sold by Browder falls apart.

Moreover, Magnitsky was not the first to report the fraudulent tax scheme against the Russian Treasury; someone else was. Magnitsky was, however, being in-

Sergei Magnitsky

vestigated for tax fraud committed by Browder, and that investigation had begun in 2005. Not only that, but Magnitsky was never a lawyer, as Browder repeatedly claims, hired freshly in 2007. He was Browder's long-time accountant, in association with him since at least 2002, and Magnitsky devised schemes to avoid Russian taxes on Browder's earnings. The 2013 conviction of Browder for massive tax fraud shows charges against Magnitsky being dismissed. He was not convicted as a "dead man" as Browder histrionically claims.

The film shows Browder, hardly the towering epitome of righteousness, running away from process-servers in New York City who were trying to secure his appearance for a deposition—something he assiduously avoided until 2015. Shots from the videotaped deposition itself, blow further huge holes in Browder's credibility. He claimed fifty times that he couldn't remember details about the story he has told millions of times, constantly deferring to "his team," and to a trove of stolen, unauthenticated documents, admittedly gathered—if they were not forgeries—in violation of Russian and other privacy laws. Browder answered "I don't know" *211 times.* Without blinking, Browder asserts, under oath, that Secretary of State John Kerry is a Putin enabler, a Putin stooge.

Someone with the gumption to take up distribution of this film in the United States and allow its showing, inviting Browder's threatened libel suit, and prepared to finance a defense against it, would probably discover much more about British subversion of this country, and thereby perform an invaluable public service.

'Cancel the British System, Save the People'

The following transcript is an edited version of a presentation given by Will Wertz on the Aug. 11 LaRouche PAC Weekly Webcast. A video of the full interview may be found here.

Jason Ross: Today on our show we are going to have a special guest whom we will be hearing from, *EIR* Editorial Board member Will Wertz. Will is going to help us understand that there is far more to the ongoing coup attempt against the Donald Trump Presidency than what's sometimes called the "Deep State." The roots of this coup operation go beyond the bounds of the United States, and go very prominently to Britain, to the still-existing British empire. So, let's turn it over. Will, what can you tell us about the deeper implications that we should take from this attempted coup against the President? What does this mean; where is it coming from?

Will Wertz: Lyndon LaRouche made the following comment: "The American people must demand that the ongoing treasonous British coup against the U.S. Presidency and the nation itself must be stopped, and the perpetrators prosecuted and imprisoned. The British system must be cancelled, and the President must make every effort to save the people of this country and the rest of humanity from further British-directed depredations against their lives. Cancel the British system; save the people."

What I'm going to do today is to present the documentation which shows that what we have here is not a Russian interference in the domestic affairs of the United States of America, but rather a very directed interference on the part of the British empire. This is what should be

> **"What Lyndon LaRouche has called the Four Powers concept, an alliance among the United States, Russia, China, and potentially India, which represent the industrial power on this planet and the vast majority of the world's population … can solve virtually any problem with which we are faced on planet Earth … The Korean Peninsula crisis, the fight against terrorism in the Middle East and North Africa require such collaboration."**

investigated, as opposed to so-called "collusion" between President Trump's campaign team and the Russians. This is very important to document, and it's absolutely critical that this coup be stopped; because we are, at this moment in world history, on the brink of another financial breakdown, far larger than in 2008. We are in a situation where the British, to preserve their bankrupt financial system based in the City of London and in Wall Street, are committed to bringing down the U.S. President to prevent the alternative to that collapse from being realized.

The alternative to that collapse is what Lyndon LaRouche has called the Four Powers concept, an alliance among the United States, Russia, China, and potentially India, which represent the industrial power on this planet and the vast majority of the world's population. That combination can solve virtually any problem with which we are faced on planet Earth and beyond. For instance, the Korean Peninsula crisis requires the collaboration of the United States with China, and Russia; both of which are neighbors of North and South Korea. The fight against terrorism in the Middle East and North Africa, which extends even beyond those areas, requires such collaboration. The rebuilding of the world economy requires such collaboration, particularly by the United States joining the efforts initiated by China—the so-called Silk Road or the "One Belt, One Road" initiative, which Lyndon and Helga LaRouche have fought for for decades, when it was referred to as the World Land-Bridge.

All of these problems can be solved with that collaboration, and that collaboration would destroy the

Candidate Donald Trump on the presidential campaign trail.

British empire once and for all. That is what is at stake right now. I would also point out that the British empire has historically been committed to massive population reduction, genocide, reducing the world's population from the current level of more than seven billion, to one billion. That empire is willing to bring the world to the brink of thermonuclear war, with its geopolitical strategy against Russia and China. That is the underlying issue which is behind the current attempt to carry out a coup against the President of the United States.

The British Hand in Russia-Gate

The evidence of the British involvement is transparent. Donald Trump announced his Presidential campaign on June 16, 2015. An article appeared in the London *Guardian* on April 13, 2017, in which the authors say that "British intelligence first became aware in late 2015"—that is, just months after Donald Trump announced his Presidential campaign—of what they call "suspicious interactions between figures connected to Trump and known or suspected Russian agents." The title of this article is "British Spies Were First to Spot Trump Team's Links with Russia." In that article, they say that these so-called "interactions" were first uncovered by the Government Communications Headquarters (GCHQ) which is the equivalent of our NSA. They go to great lengths to point out that "It is understood that GCHQ was at no point carrying out a targetted operation against Trump or his team, or proactively seeking information. The alleged conver-

sations were picked up by chance."

They also say that the GCHQ played an early prominent role in kick-starting the FBI's Trump-Russia investigation, which began in late July, 2016. It should be recalled that the Republican Convention which nominated Donald Trump occurred on July 18-21, 2016. So, GCHQ is following Donald Trump within months of his announcement for the Republican nomination for President, and the GCHQ kick-starts the FBI investigation of Donald Trump, probably within days of his getting the Republican nomination in July of 2016. The *Guardian* article continues, saying that "The FBI and CIA were slow to appreciate the extensive nature of the contacts between Trump's team and Moscow ahead of the U.S. election. This was in part due to U.S. law that prohibits U.S. agencies from examining the private communications of American citizens without warrants. They were trained not to do this." Of course the law that they're referring to is the U.S. Constitution; which unfortunately U.S. intelligence agencies have not so closely adhered to, as was exposed by Edward Snowden.

They also then report that Robert Hannigan, head of the GCHQ, passed material in the summer of 2016 to CIA chief John Brennan, and that Brennan used this information to launch a major interagency investigation. He further briefed the Gang of Eight—that's the chairs and the ranking members of the House and Senate Intelligence Committees—in August and September, about this so-called information from GCHQ. So, what you have here is the British equivalent of the NSA, kick-starting an investigation of Donald Trump soon after the Republican nominating convention. Then, John Brennan launches an interagency investigation into a domestic affair—one wonders if it is a violation of the CIA's charter that such an investigation is being launched in the first place—and began briefing the leadership of the Democratic and Republican chairs and ranking members of the House and Senate Intelligence Committees, on this information, which even to this day is not verified.

So, this is an intervention on the part of British Intelligence into the elections. Add to this the dossier which was prepared by so-called "former" MI6 agent Christopher Steele. This has functioned as the roadmap for the FBI's investigation. Copies of it were given directly to the FBI, if not by GCHQ, by MI6. We know that John McCain gave a copy to the FBI when he was given such a copy. What do we have here in terms of Christopher

OGL/Foreign and Commonwealth Office
Robert Hannigan, adviser to the British Prime Minister.

CIA portrait
John Brennan, former CIA director.

fbi.gov
FBI deputy director Andrew McCabe.

Steele? Christopher Steele is a former MI6 operative; he worked under cover of the British Foreign Ministry in the Moscow Embassy, but was an intelligence operative. He formed a company called Orbis Business Intelligence back in 2009.

From at least 2010 on, Steele had been working with the Eurasian Organized Crime Unit of the FBI, based in New York City. In the same year that Orbis Business Intelligence was launched—2009—another company in the United States called Fusion GPS was launched—same year. As early as 2010, according to court documents, those two companies had a confidentiality agreement. So, although the public story is that Fusion GPS hired Orbis Business Intelligence to do opposition research against Donald Trump on behalf of Hillary Clinton, the reality is that these two companies have been working together since their founding in 2009, and their confidentiality agreement goes back to one year later, 2010. That confidentiality agreement is being used by Fusion GPS as a reason for not handing over information to the Senate Judiciary Committee, which has requested it with respect to this dossier.

What do we have here? We have GCHQ kick-starting an investigation through international surveillance; we have former MI6 agent Christopher Steele getting information from Russians, which in this case is not very reliable; we have the use of all of this as a roadmap for launching an investigation of the President of the United States after he was elected.

It should be pointed out that one of the key people in the FBI who has been involved in this is the former acting Director of the FBI, Andrew McCabe. He was acting director of the FBI after Comey left, and now he's been replaced by Christopher Wray. But, in his early career, McCabe was head of the Eurasian Organized Crime Unit of the FBI in New York City. Senator Grassley has sent a whole series of questions to the Deputy Attorney General, Rod Rosenstein, about Andrew McCabe, because the suspicion is that Andrew McCabe was directly involved as the handler of Christopher Steele. It should also be pointed out that at a certain point, the FBI entertained the idea of paying Christopher Steele to continue his so-called research.

The question that Grassley asks is, was McCabe involved in that situation specifically? You have to understand that Andrew McCabe is under investigation right now because he was involved in a decision that his wife, Jill McCabe, would run for State Senator in the state of Virginia against Senator Dick Black. This was arranged through Governor McAuliffe, a close supporter of Hillary Clinton, who herself at the time was under investigation by the FBI. McCabe is also believed to have been involved in the investigation of Hillary Clinton's emails. The issue here is a complete conflict of interest on the part of McCabe, who may have been the key person working at the FBI with Christopher Steele.

This is the British empire nexus that is directly involved in the operation against the President of the

United States. The purpose of it is to destroy the Presidency of the United States, so that President Trump cannot develop collaborative relations with Russia and China, in particular, in the fight against terrorism, and cannot move forward in order to bring the United States into collaboration with Russia and China on the "One Belt, One Road" perspective, which would be crucial to developing the economy of the United States using American system methods.

Geopolitics or Human Development

Ross: You discussed the difference between what the motivation would be behind a British outlook versus what America might do. Could you describe for us, or help us understand, the difference between British geopolitics and what the United States could adopt as a national policy orientation?

Wertz: Yes. British policy is a policy of geopolitics, and this is a longstanding policy. In 1919, Halford Mackinder wrote a paper entitled "The Geographical Pivot of History." What he wrote there, in summary, is as follows: Who rules East Europe commands the Heartland. Who rules the Heartland commands the World Island. Who rules the World Island commands the World. Russia is the pivot area, the heartland. Surrounding it is an area which is called the Inner Crescent, which today would be called the Arc of Crisis, as defined by another geopolitician, Bernard Lewis, who was born in Britain but later became an American citizen. That's the policy that we've been carrying out. Who rules East Europe? Think about the move eastward by NATO to the very borders of Russia. Think about the policy of regime change in the entire Arc of Crisis area surrounding Russia.

This is the policy that was implemented under Zbigniew Brzezinski during the Carter Administration. It's continuing today, with the regime change policies in Libya, and in Egypt, before it was reversed by el-Sisi against Morsi. We see it in Iraq beginning in 2003; we see it today in the attempt in Syria. Before that, we saw it in Afghanistan, and that's still a crisis today. We see it in Ukraine, today. This is the geopolitical policy of the British, which led to World War II by the way, because this was the policy of Hitler. The Mackinder policy was picked up by Haushofer, who was instrumental in defining Hitler's policy of marching East to Russia—the Soviet Union at that time. So this is the geopolitical policy which is operative today.

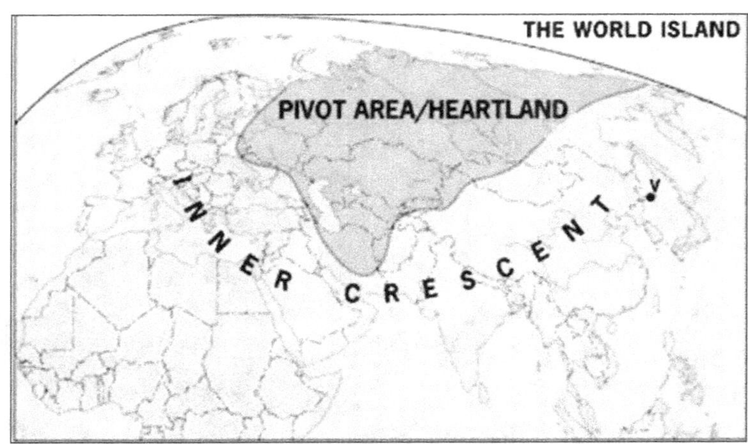

The British geopolitical view of the world as described by Halford Mackinder.

Now, contrast that to the World Land-Bridge policy. This is the policy proposed by Lyndon and Helga LaRouche. The world island is essentially Asia, Europe, and Africa. The World Land-Bridge policy is not limited to the so-called world island; this is a policy for all of humanity, extending into the Western Hemisphere. The policy is one of economic development—as the Chinese say, a "win-win" strategy, of peace based upon economic development. That is the central conception, so as to realize the actual potential of humanity for further improvements in its standard of living, its quality of mentation, and its ability not only to develop the planet Earth for man's benefit, but eventually to colonize outer space, which is man's fundamental mission.

So, these are the two contrasting views, and what Americans and others throughout the world need to know, is that the British empire is alive, and it is carrying out the same policy which it has carried out at least over the last 100 years, which led previously to world wars, and threatens to lead to world wars today. But there is an alternative, which is the World Land-Bridge, the "One Belt, One Road" policy; the Silk Road, which has been adopted by a vast majority of countries throughout the world.

Nature of the British empire

Ross: You talked about the British empire and the geopolitical objectives of Halford Mackinder. This is some time in the past. Today, I think that most people believe that there is no British empire; or that the power of the British empire has waned so dramatically from its peak that it's hardly a driving force in world affairs today. Why do you speak about the importance of the British empire? What's its power? How does it exist?

Wertz: Most people don't understand that the British empire is really based upon the Venetian system. Venice was not big in terms of military forces, or geography; it's a city. Yet, the Venetian system, as a financial system, was an imperial system, and the British system, from its inception, is modeled upon that financial imperial system. The goals of the British empire are really totally anti-human. You could compare it to the Greek mythological figure Zeus, who did not want mankind to develop; did not want mankind to have science; and did not want mankind to have technology. In opposition to that, you had Prometheus, who gave man fire—science, the means of developing the human mind so as to further the mission of humanity. The British policy is fundamentally a policy of financial imperialism, particularly after World War II, and it is also a policy based upon a perspective of destroying the notion of the sovereign nation-state, of reducing world population from the current level of over seven billion to a level of one billion or less, as I said earlier.

I want to indicate two of the leading figures in developing the British conception of empire. One is H.G. Wells, who wrote a book called *The Open Conspiracy* in the year 1928. What he said there is the following: "It lies within the power of the Atlantic communities to impose a world state, a world directorate upon the world. The open conspiracy rests upon a disrespect for national sovereignty. Its main political idea, its political strategy is to weaken, deface, incorporate, or supersede existing governments. It considers all existing governments as entirely provisional in nature." At one point he says, "There will be little need for a President." That's the policy of H.G. Wells.

As you can see, this is the policy of so-called limited sovereignty; it's the policy of supra-national institutions, like, for instance, the European Union has become. The basic idea is to eliminate national sovereignty, and create supra-national institutions in which you'd have no need for a President. Of course that's the view that the British take today. They would just as soon there not be a President who would assert the principle of national sovereignty and develop the people, through developing the economy of the nation, and working with other nations to have the same effect with respect to the world population.

Lyndon LaRouche at one point called Bertrand Russell the most evil man of the 20th Century. He's often known as an advocate of peace. Well, H.G. Wells made the same kind of argument for world peace; that was his justification for dictatorial methods. In the case of Bertrand Russell, after World War II Bertrand Russell actually proposed—when he thought the United States had a monopoly on nuclear weapons—that the United States threaten to use nuclear weapons against the then Soviet Union. He was not able to act on that idea, because as it turned out, the Soviet Union had developed nuclear weapons.

Let me just read an interchange with Bertrand Russell on this subject. He was asked, "Is it true or untrue that in recent years you advocated that a preventive war might be made against Communism, against Soviet Russia?" Russell: "It's entirely true. And I don't repent of it now. It was not inconsistent with what I think now. There was a time just after the last war when the Americans had a monopoly of nuclear weapons, and offered to internationalize nuclear weapons by the Baruch Proposal. I thought this was an extremely generous proposal on their part, one which it would be very desirable that the world should accept. Not that I advocated a nuclear war, but I did think that great pressure should be put upon Russia to accept the Baruch Proposal,

H.G. Wells

Bertrand Russell in 1936.

From left to right: Joseph Stalin, Franklin Roosevelt, and Winston Churchill at the Tehran conference on Dec. 1, 1943.

and I did think that if they continued to refuse, it might be necessary actually to go to war. At that time, nuclear weapons existed only on one side, and therefore the odds were the Russians would have given way. I thought they would." Question: "Suppose they hadn't given way?" Russell: "I thought and hoped that the Russians would give way. But of course, you can't threaten unless you're prepared to have your bluff called."

So, this is the policy of Bertrand Russell, to create a one-world directorate as in the case of H.G. Wells, and to threaten pre-emptive nuclear war against the then-Soviet Union in order to enforce such a perspective. Now we are once again on the verge of, in this case, thermonuclear war, and that is the policy of the British empire. The British basically view war as one means by which they can reduce world population.

America's Historic Enemy

Ross: In the American Revolution, the first of the complaints in the Declaration of Independence wasn't about taxation without representation; it was that the King had refused his assent to laws that were necessary for the common good. This must have shifted at some point. Now, there are so many factions in the United States who are adopting policies that sound very much like British policies. When did the United States begin to adopt an almost British outlook on foreign affairs?

Wertz: It's important for people to maintain a perspective involving a long arc of history. People know that the United States fought, before it became officially the United States and adopted a Constitution, fought a Revolution against the British empire. In 1814, it was the British who burned down the White House. This has been an ongoing conflict between the British and the United States. And when I'm referring to the British, I'm not referring to the British people; I'm referring to the British Monarchy, the British empire as a system of government. Now, the British also supported the Confederacy in the Civil War. Lincoln was assassinated at the end of that war by individuals who it is believed were actually funded by the British, specifically by one James Bulloch, the uncle of Theodore Roosevelt, who was based in Great Britain during the entire Civil War, and was essentially the foreign agent of the Confederacy based in Britain.

But the United States was able to proceed after the Civil War, and I think it became clear to the British that they were not going to be able to take over the United States by military means, but rather they had to use other means—those other means continued to involve assassination. One of the key breaking points in the whole process was the assassination of President McKinley in 1901, and of course the person who became President at that point was Theodore Roosevelt. This is in the period leading into World War I. Under McKinley, and prior to his assassination, the United States had very close relations with Germany, with Russia, and with Japan. This was reversed by Teddy Roosevelt, who established the so-called U.S.-British "special relationship." Undoubtedly, the influence of his uncle on Teddy Roosevelt played a critical role in his perspective.

Now, Franklin Roosevelt had a completely different perspective. He traced his heritage back to Isaac Roosevelt, who worked closely with Alexander Hamilton. Roosevelt's entire policy was based on the American system of economy, the same kind of American system of economy which President Trump has advocated, in recent speeches in Kentucky, Detroit, and elsewhere, including Glass-Steagall.

During World War II, the British, who had earlier backed Hitler, backed Mussolini and Franco, realized when Hitler turned westward into France and threatened Great Britain, that they needed the United States to defeat Hitler at that point. What you have from that point on, is a situation where the British operated in the United States to help bring the United States into that war.

Roosevelt's policy was always anti-colonial and

anti-empire. In 1941, there was a famous meeting between Roosevelt and Churchill— reported by Roosevelt's son, Elliott Roosevelt—in which the senior Roosevelt said, we're not fighting World War II in order to preserve the British empire, but rather, after this war we're going to use American system methods of economic development to develop the entire world and to end colonialism altogether.

When Roosevelt died in 1945, the British, through Churchill, through their intelligence agencies, and through Harry Truman, moved to begin the process of attempting to bring the United States into this British empire orbit—to reverse what Roosevelt had done—and that has been the ongoing conflict that we've had over the last seventy years or more. It's not resolved to this day, and it has to be resolved by defeating the British empire.

During World War II, the British set up intelligence operations in the United States. There was an individual by the name of Sir William S. Stephenson, Canadian-born. He set up British covert operations, which operated under the cover of the British Security Coordination, which was located in Rockefeller Center. They ran covert operations in the United States during this whole period, basically from 1939 through 1944. He represented both MI6 and MI5; he worked directly with Allen Dulles who had an office in the same building, on the same floor as Stephenson. Dulles, of course, later became head of the CIA, until he was relieved of duty by John F. Kennedy. Stephenson also worked very closely with the FBI, with J. Edgar Hoover.

In 1946, the "British-U.S. Communication Agreement" was signed as a secret treaty. It was an agreement to have intelligence collaboration between the United States and the U.K. with respect to the Soviet Union and the East Bloc

From a statue of Sir William Stephenson (code named Intrepid).

countries. This later was transformed into the "Five Eyes," which is the United States, U.K., Australia, New Zealand, and Canada. In a very real sense, the United States became a part of the British empire intelligence apparatus. And what we see today with GCHQ/MI6, their work with Brennan at the CIA, with Comey and McCabe at the FBI, and with Clapper as Director of National Intelligence, is a continuation of that U.S.-U.K. Agreement. The surveillance was done under the codename "Echelon," and it's still being done under that name, even after the Soviet Union collapsed—it's directed against the former Soviet Union and East Bloc countries.

And that is what we see today, as I said. Edward Snowden, in describing this relationship, said, the Five Eyes are a "supranational intelligence organization that doesn't answer to the known laws of its own countries." That's the picture I can give you.

What Is To Be Done?

Ross: This is a chilling picture, a very scary picture. What is it that we ought to do? This is much bigger I think, than people, even those who understand that a coup is in process or that Russiagate is a whole bunch of baloney— this is a lot deeper than what most people believe they're up against. How do we fight against this? and what do we create in its stead? What's our objective here?

Wertz: Lyndon LaRouche yesterday said that we have to "pour it on." We have to really escalate the mobilization to get a breakthrough with respect to the VIPS memorandum which we discussed at the very beginning. The whole edifice of the lie that the Russians interfered in the elections, and that the Trump campaign colluded with the Russians, is about to fall. We have to make sure that it falls. As you indicated in the beginning, the VIPS

Former CIA director Allen Dulles.

memo was produced in July, it was sent to the President, it's been sent to the Justice Department, and it's been widely circulated. We, in our movement, distributed something like one hundred copies of the VIPS memo in offices in Washington, D.C. two weeks ago, concentrating on the Intelligence Committees of both the House and Senate, as well as the Judiciary Committee. We also got this out, this week, at the Old Executive Office Building in Washington, D.C. and at the Justice Department.

The story is beginning to break: You mentioned the article in *The Nation*. This is a very powerful article that just appeared, and what the author, Patrick Lawrence, says is the following: "Under no circumstance can it be acceptable that the relevant authorities, the National Security Agency, the Justice Department (via the Federal Bureau of Investigation), and the Central Intelligence Agency leave these new findings without reply."

Now, the company that the DNC hired, Crowd-Strike, the one that claimed that it had evidence that the Russians had hacked the DNC computers, it just said, "we continue to stand by our report," arguing that by July 5, all malware had been removed from the DNC's computers. As Patrick Lawrence points out, "But the presence or absence of malware by that time is entirely immaterial, because the event of July 5 is proven to have been a leak and not a hack."

The point here is, you have *The Nation* article, you have *Newsmax*, which gave coverage to this; *Bloomberg News* had an article yesterday on the VIPS and their conclusions. What's required is for the American people to take back our country and ensure that the Constitution survives, that the republic of the United States survives. We have to mobilize to force a situation where, instead of investigating Trump, what should be investigated is the British role in all of this, and the role of members of U.S. intelligence in participating in this attempt at a coup against the United States of America and against the President of the United States of America. John Brennan recently argued that if President Trump were to fire Mueller as Special Counsel, that members of the Executive should refuse to obey his orders: That's a call for a coup by the ex-CIA director.

Lyndon LaRouche said at the beginning, we've got to cancel the British system; we've got to save our people. What's being run in this country is the equivalent of the British Opium Wars against China of the Nineteenth Century, in the opioid and other widespread drug addiction that's destroying this country. We have to free the President, to be able to carry out the policies which he at least has indicated he has an intention to implement, to the benefit of this country and the benefit of the world. That's the issue that's before us right now.

Contact the President!

What I would encourage every American citizen to do, is to contact the President: Tell him that he has your support to move on this issue. It was not a hack, it was a leak. A lie has been used as a pretext for overthrowing the President of the United States, and it's being conducted by a foreign government, in collusion with traitors in the United States like Brennan and others. Those people should be investigated. Here you have a situation where a crime was allegedly committed at the Democratic National Committee (DNC); the DNC hired its own private investigator, and that private investigator announced what the conclusion of its investigation was. The police were never invited to the scene. They never secured the crime scene, they never investigated the crime scene, and the computers have never been seen by the FBI. This is completely preposterous!

The entire country has been put in jeopardy as a result of something which is unheard of! Have you ever heard of a crime where the police were not allowed to secure the crime scene and investigate the crime? The alleged victim of the crime, who's now carrying out a campaign against the President of the United States, is allowed to determine how the investigation is conducted, and also what the conclusion of the investigation is.

This is intolerable! As Patrick Lawrence wrote in *The Nation,* it cannot stand, that there is not a reply. The forensic evidence is solid. It has been presented by experts from the NSA itself, who know how this is done.

We have to ensure that this lie collapses immediately, that the people involved in this coup against the President are investigated, and imprisoned if found guilty. That is what's required. So contact the President, tell him that you support him in going public with this. Demand that the representatives of the VIPS be allowed to testify before the various committees of Congress, to get to the bottom of this crime, which has been committed against our President and against our country.

If we do that, then we create the basis for collaboration between the United States, Russia, China, and India, which, as Lyndon LaRouche said in his Four Powers concept, is the necessary means for dismantling the British empire once and for all. What we need to do, is to destroy Zeus and free Prometheus.

JULY 14, 1996

Leibniz from Riemann's Standpoint[1]

by Lyndon H. LaRouche, Jr.

Georg Friedrich Bernhard Riemann (1826-1866)

Gottfried Wilhelm Leibniz (1646-1716)

Johannes Kepler (1571-1630)

Reprint of an article previously pubished in Fidelio *magazine, Vol. V, No. 3, Fall, 1996.*

One who has not merely learned, but knows relevant features of the work of Johannes Kepler, Gottfried Leibniz, Carl Gauss, and Bernhard Riemann, must be appalled by the unbridgeable gulf between the actual work of those exemplary, leading figures of modern European science, and what most of today's relevant academic specialists misrepresent crucial elements of that work to have been. Such has been the present writer's cumulative experience, over those sixty-odd years, since he began systematic studies of the putatively leading European philosophers from the Seventeenth and Eighteenth centuries.

During most of those decades, the writer has wrestled with relevant, published scholarly and other misrepresentations, in his verbal and oral exchanges with relevant professors and students of philosophy, with ordinary laymen, and with practitioners of mathematical

---

1. Unless otherwise noted, the references to Leibniz's writings cited here, are limited to the following: Gottfried Wilhelm Leibniz, *Philosophical Papers and Letters,* ed. by Leroy Loemker (Boston: Kluwer Academic Publishers, 1989); G.W. Leibniz, *Monadology and Other Philosophical Essays,* trans. by Paul and Anne Martin Schrecker (London: McMillan, 1965); G. W. Leibniz, *Theodicy,* trans. by E.M. Huggard, ed. by Austin Farrar, 5th printing (Peru, Ill.: Open Court Publishing Co., 1996). The principal reference to the work of Bernhard Riemann, is to Riemann's 1854 habilitation dissertation, *Über die Hypothesen, welche der Geometrie zu Grunde liegen* ("On The Hypotheses Which Underlie Geometry"), in *Bernhard Riemanns Gesammelte Mathematische Werke,* ed. by H. Weber, reprint of (Stuttgart: B. G. Teubner Verlag, 1902) [(New York: Dover Publications, 1953) and (Vaduz, Liechtenstein: Saendig Reprint Verlag)], pp. 272-287. Various English translations of this habilitation dissertation are extant, but, for purposes of precision, reference is made to the German. Other references to Riemann's writings are always to the reprint of the Weber edition: Riemann *Werke.* As a general, recurring reference, see Ralf Schauerhammer and Lyndon H. LaRouche, on Kepler and Riemann, respectively, in the "Riemann Refutes Euler" feature, in *21st Science & Technology,* Vol. 8, No. 4, Winter 1995-1996, *passim.*

science. With rare exceptions, whenever any among these crucial issues of principle is addressed, nearly all among the professional opinions encountered, are not merely mistaken, but are uttered with shameless unconcern for truthfulness.

If one applies the method of Socratic dialogue, seeking to smoke out the underlying, axiomatic roots of these differences, two causes for the widespread academic, and popular misrepresentation of Kepler, Leibniz, and Riemann, are brought to the surface. First, that the standpoint of most of those commentators, is that of Aristotle, or the empiricists. Second, when the core of the difference is chased back to its relevant epistemological rabbit-hole, any reference to the fact, that the issue is rooted in opposition to the principles underlying the scientific method of Kepler, Leibniz, and Riemann, evokes their modern opponents' implicitly hysterical effort to deny the fact, that their own, contrary, judgments are derived from such differences in axiomatic assumptions.

Typically, the hysteria expressed on the second count, is of the same form as Isaac Newton's absurd literary outburst: ... *et hypotheses non fingo!* The Newtonian system rests upon a very precisely defined hypothesis, which Newton denies to exist.[2] On the subject of Kepler, Leibniz, or Riemann,[3] the argument of most putative scholarly authorities, is analogous to Newton's denial of the existence of his own hypothesis. Rather than acknowledging the difference between their own and their subject's axiomatic assumptions, Newton *et al.* have insisted, that they themselves have no such assumptions to be contested. That hysterical behavior by Newton, *et al.*, might remind us, of the startled, wild-eyed boy (probably the local schoolyard bully) caught by his mother at the moment he has his hand in the cookie-jar, with inculpatory crumbs all around his mouth, shrieking at his mother: "What cookie-jar!"

As we shall show in the course of this paper, those writers against whom we complain thus, have not re-lived the Socratic experience of the fundamental discoveries achieved by any among these three crucial figures of modern science. We shall show, that, for that reason, however much they might claim to have learned, they have no direct mental experience of the relevant acts of discovery of principle involved. Thus, however much they have merely learned, they know relatively nothing of crucial importance about those types of subject-matters of science, in which the principal variables to be considered, are differences in underlying (e.g., axiomatic) assumptions.

Thus, one might recognize, as in the manner indicated above, that the seemingly characteristic trait among today's roster of putatively authoritative commentaries, is that each and all are governed much less by a passion for truth, than by blind zeal. We observe that that zeal is commonly mustered in defense of some philosophical standpoint contrary to that of any and all among of such targets of their muddled commentaries, as those four whom we have listed at the outset of this paper. In general, it may be said, that most such commentators are fairly classed, either as Aristoteleans, or philosophical empiricists. All seek to deny, that any influential principle of mathematics or physics (for example) might have been achieved by a scientific method contrary to their own.[4] Above all, they reject that fundamental principle of Socratic method, Plato's method of hypothesis, by means of which all of the crucial discoveries of Kepler, Leibniz, and Riemann (for example) were generated.

For that, and related reasons, no competent representation of the central conceptions underlying Leibniz's work can be presented in the terms of scholarship which have, unfortunately, become conventional in qualifying doctoral candidates, or, more generally, in the production of related, putatively "scholarly" theses. In the case, such as this topic, in which most among the putative authorities are distinguished almost as much by their incompetence (or intellectual dishonesty), as their scholarship, one must emulate that most estimable Franciscan, François Rabelais, to reject, as ridiculous,

---

2. See Riemann *Werke*, pp. 525: *Die Unterscheidung, welche Newton zwischen Bewegungsgesetzen oder Axiomen macht, scheint mir nicht haltbar. Das Trägheitsgezetz ist die Hypothese: Wenn ein materieller Punkt allein in der Welt vorhanden wäre und sich im Raum mit einer bestimmten Geschwindigkeit bewegte, so würde er diese Geschwindigkeit beständig behalten.* An English translation of this is found in the translation of the "Philosophical Fragments" from the Riemann *Werke*, published in *21st Century Science & Technology*, Vol. 8, No. 4, Winter 1995-1996, p.57. More on the hypothetical basis for Newtonian physics, below.

3. Hereinafter, we focus upon these three figures of the four listed. Our primary focus here, is the retrospective connection of Riemann to Leibniz. Kepler is kept in focus, for reasons to become clear later in the paper. Gauss, the most prolific mind in modern science after Leibniz, represents, together with his collaborator Wilhelm Weber, and protégé, Riemann, a topic deserving of special attention in a location devoted to that connection.

4. As James C. Maxwell purported to justify his refusal to acknowledge the work of the Gauss, Weber, and Riemann which Maxwell had parodied. He explained, that it was his policy to refuse to recognize the existence of any geometries but "our own."

the suggestion, that consensus among a representative body of putative scholarly authorities, such as our modern Suckfists and Kissbreeches of science, might be the relevant approach to the issues at hand. One must reconstruct the relevant principles, as if from the ground up. To this end, as we have said above, one must follow the map of Plato's method of negation of axiomatically misguided, but official, or other generally held opinion; we must employ the Socratic method of hypothesis.

Today, the most efficient standpoint from which to present, to a modern, literate audience, the axiomatic basis for Leibniz's scientific work, is the case of the fundamental discovery, respecting the principle of hypothesis, which Bernhard Riemann applied to mathematical physics, in his 1854 habilitation dissertation.[5] This present writer's discoveries within the domain of Leibniz's science of physical economy, provides the best vantage-point from which to demonstrate this specific connection of Leibniz to Riemann. We summarize that approach to the conceptions; we, thus, avoid the wide, textbook-paved road to Hell, and follow the Classical humanist method, instead. The latter, is the method of re-experiencing, at least in outline of the crucial points, the mental processes of one or more among the relevant original discoverers. The relevant case here, is the present writer's re-enactment of Riemann's discovery, but from a fresh standpoint. This serves, in turn, as our vantage-point for pointing out some characteristic features of Leibniz's method.

Three points are considered below. First, what the present writer came to recognize as the deeper significance of Riemann's habilitation dissertation. Second, how the writer's own discovery in physical economy imparts to Riemann's discovery, an otherwise overlooked authority. Finally, how we are forced, by considering Riemann's and the writer's own discoveries, to adopt a deeper appreciation of some among the more celebrated writings of Leibniz.

1. The Principle of 'Universal Characteristics'

During the interval from his own fourteenth through eighteenth birthdays, this writer became a follower of Gottfried Wilhelm Leibniz. His acquaintance with Leibniz came through English editions of some of Leibniz's noted books, obtained, chiefly, either from the

family household's library, or the Lynn, Massachusetts Public Library. This came as part of a project begun the summer preceding the writer's thirteenth birthday, and continued through his eighteenth year: a comparative study of the relatively most popular titles from leading English, French, and German philosophers of the Seventeenth and Eighteenth centuries, taking each in chronological order.

The writer began with writings of Francis Bacon, turned next to Thomas Hobbes, René Descartes, John Locke, Leibniz, David Hume, Bishop George Berkeley, Jean-Jacques Rousseau, taking up English translations of Immanuel Kant's *Critique of Pure Reason* and *Prolegomena to Any Future Metaphyics* about two and a half years later. The Leibniz writings featured in this series (and read, over and over again), were the *Monadology, Theodicee,* and *Clarke-Leibniz Correspondence.*[6] At that time, the writer then found the empiricists trivial in content, relative to Leibniz, although foes of some importance respecting their obvious influence on the world as viewed from 1930's Massachusetts. It was the defense of Leibniz against the central argument of Kant's *Critique of Pure Reason,* which proved itself a more worthy and profitable challenge, back then. Although this writer did not turn to a systematic study of Plato's writings until the mid-1950's, he had already been steeped in Plato's method of hypothesis, through studying and defending certain among the leading published writings of Leibniz.

Obviously, as for any person, many childhood and youthful experiences converged to shape the present writer's character. However, in retrospect, the importance of working through a pro-Leibniz counter-attack upon Kant, was, without doubt, the most crucial of these formative experiences. This influence was hewn into a practical form by his most significant post-war experience, the encounters with, first, Norbert Wiener's *Cybernetics,*[7] and, also, those notions of "operations research" and "systems analysis" converging upon the work of Bertrand Russell's devotee, John Von Neumann. The earlier wrestling against Kant, provided the standpoint from which to identify the kernel of evil implicit in Wiener's statistical definition of "information theory."

As reported in various locations, by the beginning of the 1950's, the writer's original discoveries, effected

---

5. See footnote 1.

6. See footnote 1.

7. Norbert Wiener, *Cybernetics* (New York: John Wiley & Sons, 1948). The writer's first encounter with Wiener's book occurred during Winter 1948, prior to the Wiley release of the hardbound U.S. edition, in the form of a loan to him of an earlier, Paris, paperbound printing.

in the course of refuting "information theory," impelled him to undertake a careful rereading of Riemann's habilitation dissertation. The crucial importance of that rereading, lay in Riemann's addressing the subject of the determining function of Plato's method of hypothesis, in defining any competent form of mathematical physics.[8] Once we have considered the implications of Riemann's work, we are able to see his most famous predecessors within modern science in a fresh way: Gauss, Leibniz, and Leibniz's crucial predecessors, Kepler, Leonardo da Vinci, and da Vinci's crucial predecessor, Nicolaus of Cusa. Consider the relevant, central implications of Riemann's habilitation dissertation, and then the significance of Riemann's discovery, when it, in turn, is situated within the context provided by this writer's own original discoveries in physical economy.

Briefly, the significance of Riemann's discovery, is this. Consider the form of algebra introduced to the Seventeenth century by the founder of the "Enlightenment," the atheistic Servite monk, and follower of William of Ockham, Paolo Sarpi. Consider the expression of this in the work of such Sarpi lackeys and followers as Galileo Galilei, Thomas Hobbes, and René Descartes. The proximate source of the Enlightenment forms of algebra, employed by Descartes, Newton, and their devotees, is derived from an "Ockhamite" reading of what is most widely recognizable as that modern classroom parody of Euclid's geometry embedded in the mathematics curricula generally, as presented, still, in secondary and higher education during the time of this writer's youth, and earlier.

The fallacies of this algebra, are the starting point of Riemann's dissertation. His point of departure there, is that in the form of algebra derived hereditarily from the work of Galileo, Descartes, Newton, *et al.*: *Discrete events, and their associated movements, are situated within a Cartesian form of idealized space-time.* This point has been presented by the present author in numerous earlier locations, but, on pedagogical grounds, it must be stated again here, this time in a choice of setting appropriate to the connection we are exposing, between

the ideas of Riemann and his predecessor Leibniz.

Riemann opens his dissertation, with two prefatory observations. First, that, until that time (1854), "from Euclid through Adrien-Marie Legendre," it was generally presumed that geometry, as well as the principles for constructions in space, was premised upon *a priori* axiomatic assumptions, whose origins, mutual relations, and justification remained obscure. The second general point of his plan of investigation, which he restates in the conclusion of the dissertation, is that no rational construction of the principles of geometry could be derived from purely mathematical considerations, but only from experience.[9] He concludes his dissertation: "We enter the realm of another science, the domain of physics, which the subject of today's occasion [mathematics] does not permit us to enter." Riemann, thus, refutes the presumption on which a Newton devotee, of Prussia's Frederick II, Leonhard Euler, depended absolutely, for the entirety of his attack on Leibniz's *Monadology.*[10]

---

9. *Loc. cit.,* footnote 1. On the second point, Riemann writes: …*dass die Sätze der Geometrie sich nicht aus allgemeinen Grössenbegriffen ableiten lassen, sondern dass diejenigen Eigenschaften, durch welche sich der Raum von anderen dreifach augedehnten Grössen underscheidet, nur aus der Erfahrung entnommen werden können.* (pp. 272-273.) The concluding sentence of the dissertation restates this point: *Es Führt dies hinueber in das Gebiet einer andern Wissenschaft, in das Gebeit der Physik, welches wohl die Natur der heutigen Veranlassung* [the subject of mathematics] *nicht zu betreten erlaubt.* (p. 286).

10. On Euler's attack on Leibniz, see, Lyndon H. LaRouche, Jr., *The Science of Christian Economy,* (Washington, D.C.: Schiller Institute, 1987), "Appendix XI: Euler's Fallacies," pp. 407-425. Note a typographical error on p. 407; the passage should read "He [Euler] was a proponent of the Newtonian reductionist method in mathematical physics." Euler was a member of an anti-Leibniz salon within the Berlin Academy of Prussia's "Frederick the Great," closely associated with such followers of Newton's patron, Abbé Antonio Conti, and members of Conti's network of salons, as Pierre-Louis Maupertuis, Johann Lambert, Giammaria Ortes (the founder of "Malthusianism"), Voltaire, and Joseph Lagrange. On this attack on Leibniz by Euler, the following history is most notable. A purely geometrical proof for the fact that π is of a higher cardinality than the Plato-Eudoxus-Eratosthenes-Archimedes notion of "irrationals," was discovered by Nicolaus of Cusa (*cf., De Docta Ignorantia,* 1440). The physical proof, that non-algebraic (i.e., transcendental) functions must supersede the algebraic notions of Descartes and Newton, was demonstrated by Leibniz, Jean Bernoulli, *et al.,* during the 1690's, in respect to the interconnected facts of isochronicity in the gravitational field (Christiaan Huyghens) and the relativity of a constant "speed of light" with respect to refraction (Ole Rømer, Huyghens, J. Bernoulli). Using the same false premises which he adopted for the attack on the *Monadology,* Euler presumed that the distinction between algebraic and non-algebraic ("transcendental") functions could be degraded to its relatively degenerate expression, as a subject of infinite series (see *Leibniz-Clarke Correspondence* on the subject of dif-

---

8. Lyndon H. LaRouche, Jr., "On LaRouche's Discovery," *Fidelio,* Vol. III, No. 1, Spring 1994. The use of the argument supplied in Riemann's habilitation dissertation, enabled the writer to solve the problem of mathematical representation incurred by his own original discovery in the science of physical economy. Hence, because of this relationship of Riemann's discovery to his own, the result came to be identified as "The LaRouche-Riemann Method." On Riemann's habilitation dissertation, see footnote 1.

On grounds of the principles of Classical humanist, or cognitive pedagogy,[11] the prudent course of action, now, is to reconstruct the conceptions at issue from the initial standpoint of simple, deductive theorem-lattices. This pedagogical approach leads us by the most direct route, to the central issue of Riemann's discovery: *the validation of an axiomatic-revolutionary quality of discovery of universal principle, by reason of which we are obliged to construct a new mathematical physics, to su-*

persede that erroneous one previously in vogue. Later, continuing that process of construction, to the point of examining the writer's own original discovery in physical-economy, we identify the cognizable feature of the individual person's mental life, in which we may then locate the significance of Riemann's revolution in mathematical physics.

Riemann's Principle of Hypothesis

The pedagogical reference-point throughout this paper, is the contrast between that Platonic principle of *change,*[12] on which both Riemann's and the writer's own discoveries were premised, and the sterile formalism of the Aristotelean or quasi-Aristotelean models of an ordinary, deductive form of theorem-lattice. In all cases considered here, the notion of theorem-lattice is defined, and examined from the standpoint of Plato's Socratic method, by the so-called method of hypothesis.

A simple, deductive form of theorem-lattice, is defined by a process of successive approximations, as follows. Given, any set of theorems which are assumed to be not-inconsistent with one another. This presumes that the Socratic method of Plato would be able to adduce certain minimal, but sufficient, underlying assumptions, the which these theorems share in common. If so, these assumptions then constitute a set of interdependent terms, in the form of axioms, postulates, and definitions, none of which are deductively inconsistent with any among the previously given, mutually not-inconsistent theorems. Implicitly, therefore, there might

---

ferential calculus and infinite series). Around this, the Newtonian devotees, following Euler and Johann Heinrich Lambert, built the myth that the proof of π's transcendental quality, is the proof derived, "hereditarily," from the tautologically fallacious assumptions of Euler's 1761 attack on the *Monadology.* Hence, the popularization of the myth, that it was Ferdinand Lindemann, in 1882, who first "proved" the transcendental quality of π! (See Lyndon H. LaRouche, Jr., "Kenneth Arrow Runs Out of Ideas, But Not Words," *21st century Science & Technology,* Vol. 8, No. 3, Fall 1995; see reference to the π controversy, under the subhead "Axiomatic Method," pp. 43-44. See also, LaRouche reply to a critic of this section of that paper, in Letters, *21st Science & Technology,* Vol. 9, No. 2, Summer 1996.

11. The "Classical humanist" method in education has two leading features which might be treated as the definitional distinctions of that method. "Classical" should be understood, in first impression, as implying a foundation in what are identified as the "Classical," as distinct from "Archaic" (for example) plastic and non-plastic art-forms of Classical Greece. In literature, this implies the Homeric epics, and the tragedies of Athen's Golden Age. In science, it implies Plato's Socratic method of hypothesis, as typified by Plato, Eudoxus, Theaetetus, Eratosthenes, and, implicitly, also, Archimedes. Overall, it signifies the struggle of the Ionian city-states and the tradition of Solon of Athens, in combatting both the Babylonian tradition, expressed as the Persian Empire, and, also, the usurious cult of Gaia-Python/Dionysos-Apollo at Delphi (and, later, pagan Rome). In art, science, and history, it implies the principle of *agapē,* as defined by Plato and the Christian apostles, as in the *Gospel* of John and the *Epistles* of Paul. The use of these Classical Greek referents, including the Christian *New Testament,* is the significance of a Classical-humanist secondary education for the relevant medieval European teaching orders, such as the Brothers of the Common Life, the continuation of that standard of literacy among the proponents of the original (anti-Justice Antonin Scalia) intent of the U.S. Federal Constitution, and the reforms of education in Germany designed by Friedrich Schiller and his followers Wilhelm and Alexander von Humboldt. This exemplary significance of that use of the term, "Classical," extends to the principle, that all of those discoveries of principle which have been proven to be valid, as such discoveries, from all currents of humanity, non-European as European, ought to be replicated mental experiences of discovery within the minds of all prospective secondary graduates, as a precondition for citizenship, in a durable form of society. The Classical currents of philology, as those with which the Humboldt brothers were associated in their time, illustrate the manner in which the notion of "Classical" is to be extended in choice of referents, from Classical Greece, to mankind as a whole. It is the emphasis on recreating the experience of the original discovery of principle, within the mind of each pupil, which distinguishes a cognitive education, from the evil of John Dewey and the "New Math," in particular, and from today's more popular textbook, or even worse standards, in general.

12. Once one has worked one's way through the sets of later dialogues of Plato, it becomes clear, that his *Parmenides* serves implicitly as a prologue to all of those dialogues; it poses the crucial, ontological paradox, which the other dialogues address, each in its own respect. For this purpose, the *Parmenides* should be read as if it were the prefatory chorus of a tragedy, modelled upon the tragic principle characteristic of Aeschylos' work. One might apply Friedrich Schiller's explication of the principles for design of a tragedy: from opening *germ,* through *punctum saliens,* to conclusion. In the dialogue taken as a whole, the character Parmenides fails as pitiably as Shakespeare's Hamlet. The character Parmenides, like his real-life image, can not comprehend the notion of *change* as an efficient principle, just as Hamlet identifies the same cause for his own, oncoming doom, in the famous Act III, Scene 1 soliloquy. This is *change* as Heraclitus references its definition; so, for Plato, and for Riemann, the elementary form of efficient existence, is not objects akin to the notion of objects of sense-perception, but, rather, the principle of *change,* which brings such secondary phenomena as mere, apparently fixed objects, into being. *Change,* so referenced, has the connotation of *generate* or *create.* That is key to any competent reading of Plato, of Cusa, of Kepler, of Leibniz, of Riemann, or this writer's own original discoveries of the same efficient principle in physical economy.

exist an indefinite number of other theorems, none of which is inconsistent, deductively, with the same set of axioms, postulates, and definitions. The combined set of all such theorems, both known and possible, constitutes a simple theorem-lattice.

For the purpose of defining essential terms: The set of underlying, interdependent axioms, postulates, and definitions, underlying any such theorem-lattice, is the elementary, deductive form of an *hypothesis.* That is the definition of "hypothesis" employed by Plato, Leibniz, Riemann, and the present author.

If, then, there exists some stubbornly real condition or event, which were not consistent with that hypothesis, then there is no proposition based upon that condition or event, the which could be the basis for a theorem of any theorem-lattice corresponding to that hypothesis. However, if, nonetheless, all of the theorems of the first theorem-lattice correspond to actually existing conditions or events, then, there exists a new hypothesis, which defines a new theorem-lattice, for which a proposition corresponding to the newly discovered condition or event, is a valid theorem. However, no theorem of the new theorem-lattice is consistent with any theorem of the first theorem-lattice.

The discovery of the change in hypothesis, which enables the leap from the old, failed theorem-lattice, to the new, is, thus, conveniently described as the discovery of a valid, *axiomatic-revolutionary* principle.

There is a crucial, corollary point to be taken into account, in reading, and rereading the highly significant, immediately preceding paragraphs. The proposition which we might construct, as our conscious representation of a condition, or event, is not the condition, or event, which may, in our opinion, have prompted the relevant proposition. This is a scientific matter, but one which is also brought to our attention by some relatively common, non-scientific, experiences of the layman's daily life.

For example. On this account, we must become uneasy in our seats, when some typical, philosophically illiterate person insists, that he, or she, is, in the words of Hollywood's "Sergeant Joe Friday," insisting upon "Just the facts, Ma'am." For example, what the attorneys and judges, in a legal proceeding, insist are "facts," *are not reality per se,* but merely a special kind of subjective assessment, which might, or might not, have relevant correspondence to the reality to which the proceeding is putatively addressed.

To this point: Even if we might be persuaded, that

we have overcome the hurdles of sincerity, in assessing a witness's report, the fact that the witness might be presumed to be speaking *sincerely,* and in his or her best judgment, does not rise to the standard for presuming, that the witness is also speaking *competently* of what that witness imagines himself, or herself to have experienced. Usually, the most favorable assumption which might be suggested, in the case of virtually any witness, is that the significance of a truthful effort to state a fact, or facts of a matter, is, that *it represents the present limits of the subject's competence to interpret what the subject believes to have been the experience of his, or her senses.*

"Truthful," when employed, carelessly, as a synonym for "sincerity," does not mean "real." What may qualify as a "fact," or "evidence," by extant legal or other professionals' standards, does not necessarily signify "true," "truthful," or "real," even if the relevant utterance is the most sincere which the subject might utter on the matter of the event being considered.[13]

---

13. In the line of discussion being developed here, we have already put to one side the substitution of non-existent conditions or events, for real ones. Three distinct classes of such substitutions are notable among those excluded from consideration in this portion of the text. (A) Simple lies. (B) Sophistries derived, as conclusions, from wishfully altered hypotheses. For a simple example: "I do not like him, therefore, I choose to find plausible anything bad said of him, and profess to consider as incredible, anything which might work to his credit." (C) Fallacies of composition superimposed, like a Procrustean Bed, upon perceived reality, to the purpose of protecting either an hypothesis, or some specific, isolated belief. Illustration: the principal origin of spread of gnosticism within western European Christianity, is the legalization of Christianity, as part of the Roman pagan Pantheon, by the Emperor Constantine. The most important action to this effect, was the later Byzantine emperors' virtual, or actual banning of the Plato who had been the correlative of Christian theology, and the introduction of Plato's adversary and bellwether of oligarchical social order, Aristotle, as authorized replacement. The efforts of the powerful oligarchical families, to defend their feudal and financier-aristocratic privileges, despite Christianity, has been the continuing source of renewal of the corrupting influence, within the clergy and churches, of the gnosticism inherent in Aristotle's philosophy and method. To avoid the embarrassing truth about the origins of gnosticism, the myth was created, that it was the Jews who are chiefly responsible for introducing gnosticism to western Europe, as via "Averroesism." This apology for oligarchism of both the landed and financier oligarchies—and, Aristotle, has been, thus, the most common source of religious anti-semitism. On the other hand, Friedrich Nietzsche, like his follower Adolf Hitler, premised his argument for ridding Europe of Jews, on the charge that it was the Jews whose collective crime had been the establishment of Christianity. Similarly, another illustration of category (C) taken from real life: To defend the Venice-created cult of Isaac Newton, Leonhard Euler, and many other devotees of the Newton cult, were willing to go to any lengths, as did J.C. Maxwell and Hermann Helmholtz, to defend the hypothesis of their cult's demi-god. Or, for a

In the language of simple theorem-lattices: In the case, that some evidence forces us to abandon one hypothesis, for another, only the valid evidence prompting the theorems of the first theorem-lattice, but not the theorems themselves, are carried forward as evidence addressed by theorems of the second lattice. Virtually none of the theorems of the old lattice are incorporated in the new; virtually all of the theorems which, in the first lattice, were associated with the carried-forward experimental evidence, are abandoned by the second lattice, as inconsistent with truth.

Truthfulness, in science, or in ordinary testimony, lies not in what the witness believes he, or she has seen, heard, touched, felt, tasted, or smelled; truthfulness lies in the choice of hypothesis, which underlies those subjective things, called propositions, which the witness has constructed as much, or more, from his, or her prejudices, as from the relevant experience. This is to be said in the same sense, as to argue, that where a member of an illiterate culture recognizes no more than "rock," a representative of a literate culture recognizes "ore." Or, to say, that the representative of the illiterate culture sees the stars moving about us; whereas, the representative of the literate culture, such as that of Plato's Academy of Athens, sees the moon orbiting the Earth, and the Earth rotating, while orbitting the sun.[14]

Riemann makes clear, in his referenced dissertation, that his emphasis upon experience, does not signify the popular delusion of the illiterate persons: The delusion that what we know as factual, is what we believe that we have experienced through our senses. Rather, the point of his argument there, is that the truthfulness of our opinions respecting actual experiences, depends, absolutely, upon the validity of the axiomatic assumptions which govern the way in which we form propositions and theorems in response to promptings of experience. It is on this point that Riemann focuses his devastating refutation of both Aristoteleanism and empiricism.

Riemann's exposure of the fraud embedded in the taught geometry and physics of both the Aristoteleans and empiricists, renders transparent the issues listed above.

The simple space-time employed by Galileo, Descartes, Thomas Hobbes, Robert Hooke, Newton, *et al.,* was based on certain, *a priori,* axiomatic assumptions respecting extension in four, mutually independent senses of direction, three of extension in space, and one in time: a "quadruply-extended space-time manifold." It was assumed, *a priori,* that space is extended without limit, and in perfectly uninterrupted continuity: backward-forward, up-down, side-to-side. It was assumed, *a priori,* that time is extended, similarly, backward and forward. It was assumed, *a priori,* that place, size, and movements of events can be situated mathematically, as though these were something plopped into what were otherwise an empty, continuous, space-time void.[15]

---

concluding example of this most relevant problem: The babbling fool who insists, that, since Karl Marx approved the idea of a progressively graduated income-tax, in the *Communist Manifesto,* that a man as fascistic as that "Miniver Cheevy" of the Confederacy's "Lost Cause," Ku Klux Klan fanatic and U.S. President Woodrow Wilson, was a Communist. Under "Lost Cause" devotee J. Edgar Hoover, the FBI was riddled with precisely such fanatical fools of the Roy M. Cohn breed.

14. These elementary considerations respecting solar phenomena, underscore the fact, that any university which tolerates a policy of eliminating, or minimizing the student's requirement for mastery of the work of "dead white European males," is clearly guilty of perpetrating a fraud upon both the students, and those institutions of society, including government, to which that university presents its graduates as competently educated. Exemplary is the fairy-tale, repeated by many illiterates with university bachelor and even terminal credentials, who believe in the myth of the "Copernican Revolution," that Mesopotamian lunatic calendars preceded solar calendars, and that the best astronomy, prior to Copernicus, was that of the fraud concocted, for ideological purposes, by Claudius Ptolemy. India's Bal Gangadhar Tilak was only citing already extant astrophysical and scholarly evidence, when he reported, in his *Orion,* that the Vedic solar astronomical calendars of Central Asia, circa 6,000-4,000 B.C., were already vastly more advanced scientifically, than any of the lunar calendars later presented in Mesopotamia. A similar case is demonstrated for ancient Egypt's solar astronomy. Aristarchus, long prior to Claudius Ptolemy's concoction of his hoax, had already defined the elementary hypothesis upon which rested the modern solar astronomy of such as the pre-Copernicus (1473-1543)

Nicolaus of Cusa (1401-1464). Every competent program of combined secondary and higher education, requires a student's mastery of the work in mathematics, astronomy, and philosophy, by Thales, Plato, Theaetetus, Eudoxus, Euclid, Aristarchus, Eratosthenes, and Archimedes, through the construction, by Cusa's collaborator, Paolo Toscanelli (1397-1482) of the world map, which Christopher Columbus acquired through the Portugal-based executor of Nicolaus of Cusa's estate, and upon which Columbus largely relied, for his planning his first, 1492, voyage to the Americas. Most of the ideas underlying modern science, in every country, are derived chiefly from the original discoveries in geometry and scientific method, which we have inherited, chiefly, from such representatives of the Classical Greece tradition as these. As in astronomy, so, in general, the truthfulness of any report of a condition or event, lies in the hypothesis which has governed the manner the revelant experience has been comprehended by the mind of the witness. "Truth in education" cannot exist, without prompting the student to reenact, in his, or her mind, the act of original discovery by those ancient Greek and other individual minds, to which our civilization is largely indebted for the development of those hypotheses upon which the truthfulness of contemporary judgment depends, without exception.

15. *Cf.* Riemann, *Plan der Untersuchung, Werke,* pp. 272-273.

To these arbitrary, *a priori* assumptions, other assumptions of a physical nature were similarly attached. Those persons who might be classed as "materialists," presumed, not only that these assumptions about space-time were products of the senses, but that the relevant features of sense-perceptions were mirror-images of the real world external to our senses. Others, such as the empiricist followers of Sarpi, Galileo, Hobbes, *et al.,* did not presume that sense-perceptions were necessarily mirror-images of the world outside our skins; however, from the standpoint of the pervasive fallacy intrinsic to popular misconceptions of physical space-time, still today, Riemann's dissertation applies equally to all among the Aristoteleans, materialists, and empiricists.

Riemann's argument against that view of physical space-time, is predominantly twofold. First, that the referenced assumptions of Galileo, Descartes, Newton, *et al.,* were merely arbitrary assumptions. Second, that these assumptions were demonstrably false. The proof of these two arguments lay in the principle set forth by the founder of modern science, Nicolaus of Cusa, in his *De Docta Ignorantia*: the principle of measurement.

Given the topic under which this paper is subsumed, which is the retrospective view of Leibniz from the standpoint of Riemann's discoveries: The most convenient illustration of the way the principle of measurement applies, is the instance of the use which Jean Bernoulli and Leibniz made of the intersecting subjects of isochronicity (a phenomenon of gravitation) and the brachystochrone problem (refraction of light at a measurable, "constant speed"). Both of these were treated by Bernoulli and Leibniz, as arising out of the work of Christiaan Huyghens.[16] In this connection, lay the physical basis for Leibniz's insistence upon replacing the "algebraic" methods of Galileo, Descartes, and Newton, by a "non-algebraic" (transcendental) form of mathematical physics.[17]

Riemann's dissertation introduces explicitly, a conception already implicit in the work of Leibniz and others, earlier: he establishes there the replacement of Newtonian physics in space-time, by the notion of *physical space-time.*[18] He excludes the recklessly gratuitous, *a priori* assumptions of *limitless extension,* and *perfectly continuous extension.* He then attributes the principle of extension to every physical principle whose validity has been demonstrated by experimental measurement, as Rømer, in 1676, had reported his astrophysical measurement of the estimated "speed of light," and as Jean Bernoulli, twenty years later, reported the coincidence of refraction of that light and Huyghens' representation of isochronicity within the gravitational field. Thus, every validated physical principle is to be added to dimensions of space and time, as an independent dimension of a physical space-time manifold of "*n* dimensions." This arrangement excludes, axiomatically, any toleration of the Euler-Cauchy-Clausius-

---

16. See Christiaan Huyghens, *The Pendulum Clock,* trans. by Richard Blackwell (Ames, Iowa: Iowa State University Press, 1986); and Christiaan Huygens, *A Treatise on Light* (1678), reprint of English translation: (New York: Dover Publications). On Huyghens' relationship to the discovery of the "speed of light," see Poul Rasmussen, "Ole Rømer and the Discovery of the Speed of Light," *21st Century Science & Technology,* Vol. 6, No. 1, Spring 1993. On the relationship to Jean Bernoulli's solution to the brachystochrone problem, see D.J. Struik, *A Source Book in Mathematics, 1200-1800* (Princeton, N.J.: Princeton University Press, 1986), pp. 391-399.

17. This latter transformation became a central issue of the Leibniz-Clarke correspondence: Leibniz's insistence that a competent calculus could not be represented by the relatively degenerate geometry of infi-

nite series.

18. For the purposes of this paper, it should be sufficient merely to note, as we do here, that Riemannian physical space-time does not permit "linearization in the very small." On this, note the conflict between Riemann and Rudolf Clausius. In a related example, also contrast Riemann's notion of physical space-time with that presented by Princeton's Hermann Weyl. For example, in editor Heinrich Weber's appended note to Riemann's *Ein Beitrag zur Electrodynamik* [*Werke*, p. 293], Weber reports Rudolf Clausius' attack upon Riemann's function, as follows.

$$P = -\int_0^t \sum \sum \varepsilon\varepsilon' \; F\left(\tau - \frac{r}{\alpha}, \tau\right) d\tau$$

Of which, Weber reports Clausius to argue: *Die Operation, vermöge deren später dafuer ein nicht verschwindend kleiner Werth gefunden wird, muss daher einen Irrthum enthalten, den Clausius in der Ausführung einer unberechtigten Umkehrung der Integrationsfolge findet.* Thus, Clausius demands linearization in the very small. An English translation, by James Cleary, of H. Weber's note, is found in the textbook by Carol White, *Energy Potential* (New York: Campaigner Publications, 1977), pp. 299-300.

The formal-mathematical aspect of Clausius' argument is to be recognized at once as an "hereditary" influence of the same tautological fallacy on which Euler premised his 1761 attack upon Leibniz's *Monadology.* Similarly, it is the failure of Euler, Lagrange, Laplace's Augustin Cauchy, Hermann Grassmann, Rudolf Clausius, Hermann Helmholtz, *et al.,* to recognize Leibniz's argument against Venetian Abbot Antonio Conti's agent, Dr. Samuel Clarke, respecting the implications underlying the incompetency of the mere numerical approximations supplied by use of an infinite series as a substitute for an actual calculus. In the *Beitrag,* Riemann is referencing work-product of his own collaboration with Wilhelm Weber, of which more is to be learned in a forthcoming issue of *21st Century Science & Technology.* In short, Clausius' invocation of the notorious "sliding rule," is not only flatly wrong, but, reveals much more about his own, and Grassmann's mathematics, than it does respecting the work of Weber and Riemann.

Helmholtz, *et al.* notion of "linearization of physical space-time in the very small."

At the outset of his dissertation, Riemann already defends what is to appear as his construction of a multiply extended physical space-time manifold. This defense rests chiefly on two general premises. First, each discovered principle validated by experimental measurement, has, consequently, the manifest quality of extension. Second, each such principle has the quality of a dimension, in the respect of the same rule of mutual independence among dimensions, which any Euclidean form of geometry attributes to mutually independent senses of direction of dimensions of space and time.

Yet, this construction poses problems which can not be resolved within either the confines of a formal mathematics, or any extant formal mathematical physics. To resolve these further problems, one must depart the domain of mathematics, to enter the domain of experimental physics. One must enter Nicolaus of Cusa's domain of *measurement.*

There must be some experimental proof, which demonstrates, in a measurable way, that a certain crucial-experimental occurrence requires us to construct one kind of mathematical physics, rather than some other. This demonstration must have such *unique* significance. Riemann points to three hints, on which he has relied for elaborating the general quality of "yardstick" we require for that kind of measurement. Two hints are taken from the work of Riemann's patron, Professor Carl F. Gauss: Gauss's work on bi-quadratic residues,[19] and general theory of curved surfaces.[20] The

third is borrowed from Riemann's own work, the concept of *Geistesmassen* which he outlined in his posthumously published *Zur Psychologie und Metaphysik.*[21]

To be considered validated, the new physical principle must correspond to some measurable difference in the characteristic action "connecting any two points" within the reality corresponding to the choice of mathematical-physics manifold being tested. The notion of this measurable difference, is suggested by the attempt to determine whether the very large surface on which one is travelling is a plane, or a curved surface.[22] In terms of a physical space-time manifold of "*n* dimensions," it is the relative curvature of the "surface," which the crucial experiment must measure. Hence, the importance, for Riemann, of the hints supplied by Gauss's work on biquadratic residues and general theory of curved surfaces.

For Riemann's physics, one such yardstick is required. The present writer's discoveries demonstrate that two yardsticks, rather than one, are required. We shall come to that in due course, below. First, we must locate the place where Riemann's notion of *Geistesmassen* fits in; this touches the most crucial distinction of Riemann's physics, and also the unique feature from which the unique, crucial superiority of the present writer's work in economics has been derived. To that purpose, we now restate what we have just described, this time, explicitly referencing, as Riemann does, Plato's—and Leibniz's—method of hypothesis.

In place of the words "dimension," substitute such words as "axiom, postulate, definition." That is to say, recognize the equivalence of a Riemann multiply-extended, physical space-time manifold, to Plato's, Leibniz's, Riemann's, and the present author's notion of "hypothesis." The connection is highlighted by reference to Leibniz's notion of *necessary and sufficient reason,* a notion which is Leibniz's refined treatment of the notion of *reason* as this appeared in the work of that Johannes

---

19. Riemann, *op. cit.*, p. 273: ... *Gauss, in der zweiten Abhandlung über die biquadratischen Reste.* [*Theoria Residuorum Biquadaticorum: Commentatio Secunda* (1831), *Carl Friedrich Gauss Werke*, II (Hildesheim: Georg Olms Verlag, 1981). pp. 93-178. See, also *Zur Theorie der Biquadratischen Reste Werke*, II, pp. 315-385.]

20. *Ibid.*, p. 276: ... *Zu beidem sind die Grundlagen enhalten in der berühmten Abhandlung des Herrn ... Gauss über die krummen Flächen.* See, *Disquisitiones Generales Circa Superficies Curvas* (1828) Gauss *Werke,* IV, pp. 217-258. See, Gauss' notice of this paper: pp. 341-347; the crucial issue of mapping is presented on pp. 344-345. See, also, *Allgemeine Auflösung der Aufgabe die Theile einer gegebenen Fläche so abzubilden* (the famous "Copenhagen Prize Essay") (1822), pp. 189-216. Notable is the issue of mapping of an ellipsoid onto a sphere; the referenced work of Gauss' on this subject was, most immediately, a reflection of his discoveries in geodesy, in the setting of his 1818-1832 triangulation-survey of the territory of the Kingdom of Hanover. However, Gauss' work in "non-Euclidean geometry" dates not only from his earlier discoveries in astronomy, but, according to a Nov. 28, 1846 letter to H.C. Schumacher, to 1792. Notably, it was from this starting-point in the work of Gauss, not the quasi-Kantian Newton devotee and plagiarist of Niels Henrik Abel, Augustin Cauchy, that Riemann derived what

some wags amuse themselves to describe as the "Cauchy-Riemann" function; the debt to A.M. Legendre is significant, not to Gaspard Monge's and Legendre's hateful adversary, and Laplace protégé, Cauchy.

21. *Ibid.*, p. 273: ... *und einigen philosophischen Untersuchungen Herbart's, durchaus keine Vorarbeiten benutzen konnte.* For the relevant text of Riemann's earlier commentary on this, see *Werke*, pp. 509-520. For an English translation of the latter, see "Riemann's Philosophical Fragments," *21st Century Science & Technology, op. cit.*, pp. 51-55.

22. As is suggested by Eratosthenes' experimental measurement of the estimated curvature of the Earth's meridian, more than two thousand years before any person had yet seen the Earth's curvature.

Kepler, whose specified requirements for the development of a calculus were satisfied by Leibniz's work.

Proceed to that end, thus. As we proceed, now, bear in mind the following: Think of "dimension, axiom, postulate, definition," and "hypothesis," as representative of a common quality termed, alternately, either "formal discontinuity," or "singularity." Physically, each, as in the case of adding a new degree of independent dimension, signifies some break in the continuum extant prior to the introduction of such a singularity.

Consider the proposition: *What is a sufficiency of properly selected, axiomatic assumptions, respecting the task of assessing the significance of a particular event, when that event is considered primarily as a change in the state of the universe in which it occurs?* Select, as such an event, the equivalence which Jean Bernoulli demonstrated, between Huyghens' notion of the cycloid path as one of isochronicity (*tautochrone*) in Kepler's "gravitational field,"[23] and the fact that the variable feature of refraction describes the same tautochronic pathway.[24] What are the necessary and sufficient features of an hypothesis, which hypothesis defines a physical space-time in which these phenomena and their coincidence must occur? That hypothesis, whatever it may prove to be, constitutes "necessary and sufficient reason."

That reflects Leibniz's refinement of Kepler's use of the notion of *Reason*. This function of *Reason* (Kepler), or *necessary and sufficient reason* (Leibniz), is the alternative to the use of the percussive notion of "causality," as a geometrically degenerate parody of the notion of Reason, in the work of materialists, or empiricists such as Galileo, Newton, *et al.*

This leads to Riemann's notion of *unique* events, as those experimental events which force us to reconsider whatever has passed, until now, for a notion of necessary and sufficient reason, that hypothesis heretofore considered as established. The general use of "crucial experiment," as ostensibly a substitute for "unique," does not rise to the functional significance of our use of "unique" here.

Implicitly, every event is, potentially, a unique experimental event. In some circumstance, any event must implicitly overthrow the presumptions of someone's hypothesis. Obviously, we, like Riemann, Leibniz before him, and so on, are situating these and related matters within an historically specific, task-oriented setting, the interdependency between mankind's progressive mastery of the universe, and the internal development of Classical forms of art and science. Therefore, we employ "unique" to designate those events which have pivotal, historic significance for the discovery of valid, axiomatic-revolutionary principles of our universe. E.g., the critical experimental, or analogous events, which correspond to the singularities of a never-perfectly continuous extension of scientific and artistic progress.

In Riemann, this overview of scientific progress is typified by progress from a relatively valid physical space-time of "*n* dimensions," to a more powerful conception, a superior, relatively valid physical space-time of "*n+1* dimensions." In other words, from one, relatively valid hypothesis, to a superior valid hypothesis.

This central implication of the habilitation dissertation, leads us, implicitly, to reconsider the so-called "ontological paradox" of Plato's *Parmenides*.[25] Resituate the notion of a Riemann series (e.g., of surfaces of differing Gaussian curvature), of the topological type *(n+1)/n*, as implicitly defined by the habilitation dissertation. This presents us a series of hypothesis, $n = 4, ...,$ $i, i+1, i+2, ...$ What is the ordering principle of such a series? The answer is, first: some principle of valid successive discovery of hypotheses: a higher type of hypothesis, which underlies a series of hypotheses, as an ordinary, relatively valid hypothesis underlies the series of theorems represented by a theorem-lattice. Plato identifies this higher type of hypothesis, simply, as an "higher hypothesis." Hence, the title of Riemann's Platonist dissertation: "The Hypotheses Which Underlie Geometry."

As we depart one hypothesis of that series, to approach its proper supersessor, we must depart the domain of mathematical formalism, for the domain of either experimental physics, or something functionally equivalent to such a physics. These domains are to be

____

23. On this item, no scientifically literate person would introduce, as objection, the somewhat popularized nonsense, of asserting that the original discovery of gravitation was the work of Galileo, Newton, *et al.* Newton's algebraic representation of gravitation was explicitly derived, as a relatively degenerate representation, from Kepler's formulation for gravitation. For a summary of the way in which Newton's plagiarism of Kepler was constructed, see Lyndon H. LaRouche, Jr., *The Science of Christian Economy, op. cit.,* Chapter VII, Note 8 (see pp. 471-473).

24. D.J. Struik, *loc. cit.*

25. See *Proclus' Commentary on Plato's Parmenides,* trans. by Glenn R. Morrow and John M. Dillon (Princeton, N.J.: Princeton University Press, 1987), *passim.*

found, relative to formalism, within transinfinitesimally small, mathematical discontinuities, the existence of which the followers of Newton, Euler, Bertrand Russell, *et al.,* each and all, fraudulently deny.[26] Each valid, axiomatic-revolutionary discovery of principle (e.g., a formal axiom, a dimension, an hypothesis), is a singularity, which, discovered, fills the place defined by a transinfinitesimally small formal discontinuity in the fabric of the mathematical-physics being superseded.

The process by which that valid singularity is generated, can never be detailed at the proverbial "blackboard." Nonetheless, that process exists; its existence is provable, not by mathematics, but according to the principle of measurement.[27] The form in which that existence impinges upon knowledge, is the same quality of true *metaphor,* which is the distinguishing activity of all successful Classical forms of artistic compositions. The activity is known, otherwise, as "creative reason," or, "cognition," *when either term is employed to signify the quality of non-deductive mental activity typified by an original valid, axiomatic-revolutionary discovery of a principle of nature.* In physical science, this activity is typified by the successful generation of a valid new hypothesis. Riemann approaches the conceptualization of this activity of creative reason, with his use of the term *Geistesmassen.* This implication of the same principle of hypothesis, which underlies Riemann's dissertation, is the focus of Leibniz's *Monadology.*

'Psychology & Metaphysics'

That mental activity, through which principles of nature are discovered (and, recognized), and, through which artistic metaphor is generated (and, recognized), is not a subject for deductive methods. In that sense, the validation of an axiomatic-revolutionary principle can not be represented mathematically, either at the blackboard, or in kindred modes.[28] Nonetheless, like those

---

26. In every case examined, the argument against the existence of mathematical discontinuities is a parody of the tautological fallacy which Euler deployed in his attempted sodomy of 1761, against Leibniz' *Monadology.*

27. *Cf.* B. Riemann, *Über die Fortpflanzung ebener Luftwellen von endlicher Schwingungsweite, Werke,* pp. 156-175. In this paper, Riemann addressed the implications of the mistaken assumption, that the speed of sound represented an insuperable barrier to movement of a propelled projectile at higher speeds through the air medium. Out of his understanding of the physical significance of discontinuities arising in such functions, not only was the possibility of accelerated transsonic flight indicated, but, more generally, the general principle of isentropic compression. The crucial point illustrated, for our purposes, here, is that Riemann recognized that the appearance of a formal discontinuity, in the mathematical form of the design of his experiment, represented the presence of a singularity, a new principle—isentropic compression—to be entered into the validated physical principles of physical space-time. The problem which Riemann had successfully attacked, was that on which Britain's Lord Rayleigh discredited himself so recklessly on this point. Rayleigh's commentary on Riemann's *Fortpflanzung* shrieked, to the effect, that, if Riemann were right, then all of the physics of Rayleigh and the pro-Newton faction, were thoroughly bankrupt intellectually. The root of Rayleigh's consternation: the argument against Riemann's method, by such as Clausius, Grassmann, Helmholtz, Maxwell, and Rayleigh, is that the wrong view of gas theory is embedded axiomatically in those notions of percussive causality which Sarpi and his followers had embedded in the Cartesians and British empiricists. Riemann's representation of isentropic compression has important implications within applications of the LaRouche-Riemann method in physical economy. On the latter account, the present writer commissioned a translation of this paper of Riemann's, by Uwe Henke and Steven Bardwell, which appeared in the 1980 edition of *The International Journal of Fusion Energy* (Vol. II, No. 3, pp. 1-23).

28. This is the key to understanding the convoluted argument which underlies such later publications of Immanuel Kant as: *Critique of Pure Reason* (1781), *Prolegomena to a Future Metaphysics* (1783), *Fundamental Principles of a Metaphysics of Ethics* (1785), *Critique of Practical Reason* (1788), *Critique of Judgment* (1790), and *Perpetual Peace* (1795). Kant's argument is the basis for the mysticism of such Nineteenth-century neo-Kantian mystics as (implicit *Volksgeist* doctrinaire) Johann Fichte, (*Weltgeist* doctrinaire) George Wilhelm Friedrich Hegel, (*Zeitgeist/Volksgeist* doctrinaire, and Hegel ally) Friedrich Karl von Savigny, and the pathological Franz Liszt. The central feature of Kant's *Critiques,* and related writings on science, psychology, morals, and aesthetics, centers around the mystical irrationalism of his discussion of *synthetic judgment a priori.* Unlike his more radical, logical-positivist followers, such as Norbert Wiener of "information theory" notoriety, agnostic Kant is prepared to allow both God and creative reason to exist somewhere, but not to permit them to be known. Although there is a foretaste of Kant's argument in the mystical side of the gnostic René Descartes, in the notion of *deus ex machina,* the empiricists deny the existence of creative reason altogether. (See relevant writings of the neo-Kantians Wilhelm Windelband and Ernst Cassirer, for insight into the continuing distinctions between neo-Kantianism, on the one side, and empiricism and positivism, on the other.) Similarly, as a reflection of their pro-atheistic, empiricist "mind set," the pseudo-Christian gnostics of Britain deny the existence of a "divine spark of reason" within the individual person, i.e., deny both *Genesis* 1:26-30, and the Christian principles of *imago dei* and *capax dei.* It is for these same "Brutish" varieties of religious motives, that Galileo student Thomas Hobbes decreed the policy, for banning both metaphor and the subjunctive mood (e.g., *Leviathan*), which is the continuing policy-trend among empiricist and positivist species of modern-language stylists, to the present day. This streak, expressed variously as the atheism axiomatically inherent in empiricism and positivism, and as "agnosticism" among the followers of Kant, is a strictly correct reading of the import of Aristotle's method and writings. In modern Europe, this atheistic current is to be traced chiefly to Cardinal Gasparo Contarini's extremely influential teacher, the Pietro Pomponazzi of Padua, who taught, that, among the followers of Aristotle (and, of Pomponazzi), the human soul could not exist.

discovered, and empirically validated principles of science themselves, the non-deductive mental activity of creative reason (*cognition*) can be known as clearly as any object presented to our minds by sense-perception. If education is based, not on the stultifying, textbook drill-and-grill mode, of indoctrination in a secularist catechism, but, rather, upon the student's reenacting the original discoverer's act of discovery within the student's own, sovereign cognitive processes, the repeated experience of coming to know these discoveries in this way, enables the pupil to come to recognize the common form of that mental action of *change,* which is the common feature of the progress of the pupil's mind, from one hypothesis to the next.[29]

---

29. *Cf.* Lawrence S. Kubie, "The Fostering of Scientific Creativity," *Daedalus*, Spring 1962; also, *The Neurotic Distortion of the Creative Process* (Lawrence: University of Kansas Press, 1958).

Although Kubie, a rather celebrated Yale psychoanalyst, was a participant in the Josiah Macy, Jr. Foundation's notorious "Cybernetics" project, he proved himself insightful in his investigation of the reasons why some of those persons nominally among the most highly qualified, and formerly most promising academics, had proven sterile in the field of scientific creativity. Kubie's referenced works were published after the writer's structured, quality-control study of indicated patterns of behavior in formally well-qualified management consultants who tended to fail, consistently; hence, the referenced titles attracted this writer's attention. From the standpoint of the writer's own investigations, Kubie's observations in the 1962 *Daedalus* piece were on target. In the typical case of the failure-prone management consultant, in this writer's study, and in related cases, it was the case's educational successes which were, arguably, the source of his performance failures as a consultant. In his education, usually, that subject had been the kind of "nerd" who hit the books, learned the subject, passed the examination, whose opinions won the approval of his teachers, all the way to his pre-doctoral orals and written examination. The subject's mind was trapped inside that mere learning as a virtual reality. Clearly, during his education, the subject had employed his cognitive powers sometimes, but had never recognized the distinction between learning and the role cognitive processes contributed to assisting the learning process. Only rarely, would that subject rely upon thinking cognitively "in a pinch." If the subject must have been somewhat creative during the earlier phases of his education, his willingness to continue the learning process in that way would begin to wither away at a point proximate to his completing higher education. As he grew older, the growing maturity of his professional experience was accompanied by an apparent "calcification" of his cognitive potential. Under the pressure of desire for approval from actually present, or possible professional peers, he would fall back into the virtual reality of academically, and bureaucratically induced habits of Pavlovian "academic correctness." In a related type of case, the gifted experimental scientist might go stale, during the moments he is confronted with the prospect of defending mathematically, at the blackboard, or in a paper submitted to referees, what he knows, otherwise, to be his valid experimental discovery. As indicated in later paragraphs of this text, this is not

This brings us to the matter of *agapē* the emotional quality, contrasted to *erotic* impulses, which is characteristic of what we term here, alternately, "creative mentation," or "cognition."

In Plato, the term *agapē* arises as "love for justice," "love for truth." The Latin translation of Plato's notion of *agapē*, where the Greek term appears in the Christian *New Testament,* is the *caritas* which is translated as "charity" in the King James Version's English translation of the Latin edition of Paul's *Epistles.*[30] There are some well-known, if absurd, but clinically foreseeable, capriolically pornographic renderings of the term, from among devotees of the Oxbridge glosses on Plato; despite such sick minds, the intention, "love for justice and truth," is the only accurate rendering of "Platonic love." This quality of emotion, *agapē*, is associated only with a category of objects of thought which belong strictly to the category of "Platonic ideas."

The antonym for *agapē* is *eros,* the latter the quality of emotion peculiar to either objects of sense-perception, or to those words, methods, and procedures, the which are induced in individual behavior through the anti-cognitive, "sing for your supper," modes of "drill and grill."[31]

To make clear the significance of the term "Platonic ideas," the present author prefers the example of Eratosthenes' fair estimate for the length of the Earth's meridian. By aid of an ingenious, but mathematically simple experimental procedure, Eratosthenes estimated the polar diameter of the Earth within a margin of error of about fifty miles, and did this more than two thousand years before any person had seen the curvature of our planet. The several Classical Greek estimates of the distance from the Earth to the moon, including that of Eratosthenes, have the same relevance. We can not see, as objects, the actual astrophysical distances from Earth to the moon, sun, or neighoring planets; virtually all of astrophysics, and

---

merely a formal problem, but also a psychiatric problem, arising to this form through the victim's substituting the inappropriate, erotic form of intellectual motivation, where the non-erotic, agapic form of behavior is required.

30. The paradigmatic *New Testament* text is *I Corinthians* 13. Paul's meaning for the term, is fully consistent with that of Plato.

31. The student, and professional, who approaches his subject-matters like one who "sings no better than he believes necessary to gain his supper," is referenced by Friedrich Schiller as of the category of *Brotgelehrten.* That has been increasingly the characteristic of the education and standard of adult practice of professionals in general.

Eratosthenes' Method of Measuring the Size of the Earth

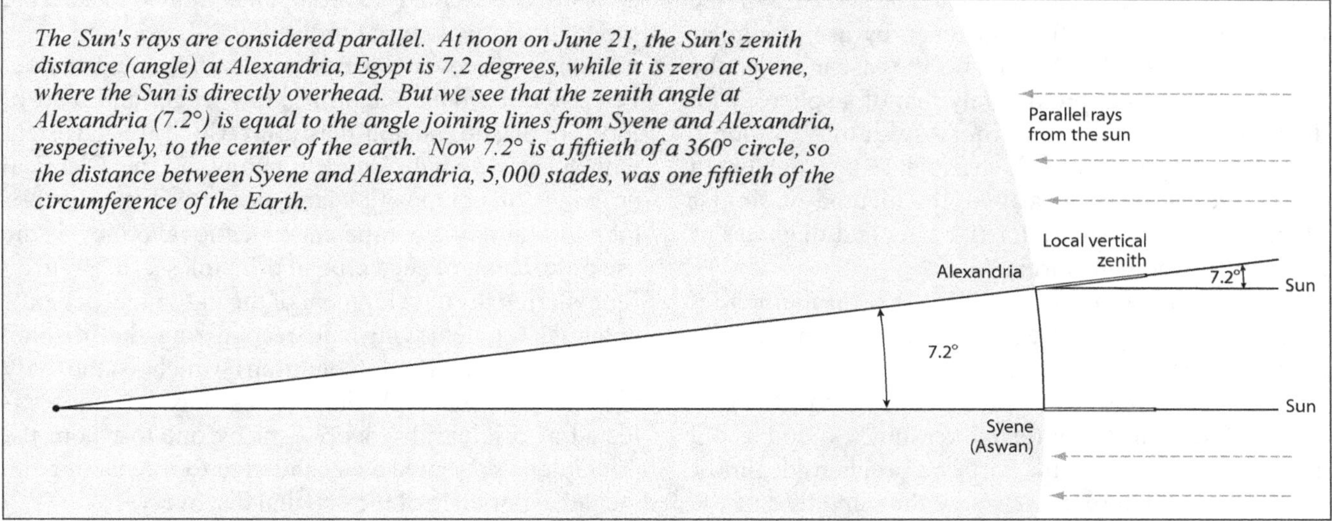

the entire domain of microphysics address objects which are not defined directly by our senses. Those matters of knowledge which lie outside simple sense-perception, fall within the category of "Platonic ideas."[32]

The distinction between living and non-living pro-cesses, and the distinction between the cognitive processes of the human individual, and the behavior of all lower forms of life, are also subject-matters which are not defined directly by our sense-perceptions. Similarly, neither "justice" and "truth," nor any validated discovery of a principle of nature, are objects defined as sense-perceptions. All of these distinctions of physical processes, which we can not define as matters of direct, simple sense-perception, but which we are able to know to be true in other ways, belong to the catgeory of "Platonic ideas."[33]

We summarize here, once again, the way in which the case of Eratosthenes' estimate of the length of the Earth's meridian presents the central role of Platonic ideas in science [See **Figure 1**].

A series of measurements is taken, by sun-dials placed at intervals along a measured (paced off) interval, along a South-North line, between Aswan and Alexandria, in Egypt. Each set of these successive series

---

32. The empiricist and positivist would argue, that such ideas are "constructs," derived, thus, from sense-perceptions. That empiricist argument, is traced to Padua's Pietro Pomponazzi through Pomponazzi's student, the Venetian Francesco Zorzi (a.k.a, "Giorgi"), who took up residence in England to serve as marriage counsellor to King Henry VIII, and served as the intellectual resource upon which the King relied, together with Venice's agent Thomas Cromwell, *et al.,* in that celebrated Anne Boleyn affair upon which the Church of England was established. Zorzi is otherwise notable in the history of England during that same period, for his direct attack on the influence of Cardinal Nicolaus of Cusa, the crucial organizer in the process leading into 1439-1440 Council of Florence, and, later, mid-Fifteenth-century canon of the Papacy. Zorzi's attack was directed against the influence of the Erasmians, the principal conveyers of the Renaissance heritage into England at that time. Zorzi demanded extirpation of the method of "docta ignorantia," and its replacement by a kind of proto-empiricism. The influence of Pomponazzi and his leading students, apart from the key role they played in orchestrating, as did Gasparo Contarini, the great schism of the early Sixteenth century, was the current of Venice's influence leading into Paolo Sarpi's founding of what we know today as the British empiricism of Bacon, Hobbes, Locke, Bentham, *et al.* Echoing Zorzi, the Sixteenth through Nineteenth centuries witnessed an hysterical effort by the followers of Hobbes, Locke, and Newton, to eliminate the notion of ideas from science and philosophy, through the establishment of the notion that those ideas were merely "constructs." The issue of infinite series, posed by Leibniz in the Leibniz-Clarke-Newton correspondence, and Euler's lunatic use of a tautological fallacy, to attack Leibniz's *Monadology,* are bellwether cases of this effort to promote the hoax of the "construct."

33. It is also stressed, in sundry other locations, that scientific knowledge requires uncovering the necessary and sufficient reason underlying the existence of the division of experience among three distinct qualities of scale, and three mutually exclusive categories of characteristic functional distinction. Of scale, we have astrophysical and microphysical, which are beyond the scope of objects perceivable to the senses, and, thus, by elimination, the macrophysical scale. Of characteristic functional distinctions, we have putatively non-living, putatively non-cognitive living, and cognitive processes. The combinations of the two types of distinctions define a simple matrix; a functionally comprehensive definition of all of the relations implicit in that matrix, is science. Thus, science as a whole does not exist outside the domain of Platonic ideas.

of measurements is taken at noon (as indicated by the sun-dials) on the same day. The angles of the shadow cast are compared. This comparison shows that the Earth's surface is not flat. However, by use of similar figures, it appears that the data fits the case in which the Earth's surface is approximately that of a sphere, with the South-North direction, from Aswan to Alexandria, corresponding to an arc of a meridian. Since the length of that arc had been measured, the method of similar figures gave an estimate for the size, and diameter of the relevant complete circle.[34]

The crucial point of describing that, in the present location, is, as stressed earlier, that Eratosthenes' defined and measured the curvature of the planet more than two thousands years before man first saw the curvature of the planet. For related reasons, Columbus did not merely suspect that the Earth was a spheroid; almost five centuries before anyone saw the curvature of the planet, Columbus knew it with scientific certainty, through work done by Toscanelli, based upon ancient Greek science, decades prior to Columbus' acquisition of the map of the planet produced by Toscanelli. The size of the planet, estimated by Toscanelli, was accurate to at least the degree of precision of Eratosthenes estimates, about 1,700 years earlier.[35] The estimates of the distance to the moon, by Eratosthenes, and Aristarchus' derivation of the demonstration that the Earth orbited the sun, are examples of the same principle of Platonic ideas.

The archetypical expression of Platonic ideas, is the quality of mental act, by means of which a valid, axi-

omatic-revolutionary discovery of a principle of nature is generated. The overriding mission of a competent policy in education, is to prompt the pupil to reenact the series of relatively more truthful, valid, axiomatic-revolutionary discoveries of principle underlying the development of both scientific knowledge, and also of forms of plastic and non-plastic art which are consistent with what we shall identify, below, as the Classical principle of composition and performance. The primary mission of a competent educational policy, is the use of teaching of such crucial principles as a "pretext" for fostering the development of the individual person's potential for deploying and recognizing that distinct quality of mental act (cognition) which is the only means by which such discoveries may be either effected as original discoveries, or by one to whom the principle is presented as a challenge for reenacting the mental experience of the original discovery.

This potential for development of the creative powers of cognition, is that distinction between man and beast underlying *Genesis* 1:26-30: mankind, male and female, made in the image of God: as Nicolaus of Cusa emphasizes, the principles of *imago viva dei* and *capax dei*. In its paradigmatic expression, as knowable to the successful student in such a Classical-humanist program of education, this act of cognition is located in the person's experience, as the quality of mental activity through which the validation of an axiomatic-revolutionary discovery of principle, is effected. In other words, the generation of a valid "leap" from a given hypothesis (theorem-lattice) to a relatively superior hypothesis. This paradigmatic act, is, therefore, the experience of higher hypothesis.

That paradigmatic experience has two distinguishable, but inseparable interdependent qualities. The occurrence of the formally validatable discovery itself, and the distinctive quality of emotion associated with that act of discovery. That latter quality of emotion, is *agapē* as Plato defines it, and as *I Corinthians* 13 also defines it.[36] It is through the summoning of the devel-

---

34. See *Selections Illustrating the History of Greek Mathematics,* trans. by Ivor Thomas, Vol. II (Cambridge, Mass.: Harvard University Press, 1980), Loeb Classical Library, pp. 266-273. Note, that Eratosthenes also supplied an estimate for the arc of a great circle passing through Alexandria and Rome. Eratosthenes' estimates are typical of the application of Classical Greek science (from Thales through Eratosthenes' time) to the methods of observation of ancient through early Ptolemaic Egypt. (The fact that Claudius Ptolemy's hoax could be tolerated by his contemporaries, illustrates the significant degeneration in scientific practice which had occurred since the deaths of Aristarchus, Eratosthenes, and Eratosthenes' correspondent Archimedes.) To gauge this, one might wisely take into account, Indo-European culture's knowledge of the long equinoctial solar-sidereal astronomical cycle, shown (by progression of positions of observed stellar constellations) to date from some time between 6,000 and 4,000 B.C. (within Orion), in Central Asia.

35. The conspicuous error in Toscanelli's map, is neither his estimated size of the planet, not the indicated distance to be spanned in crossing the Atlantic. The problem is Venetian lies respecting the distance across Asia to China and Japan, placing the latter in the middle of the United States.

36. The connection stated here is key to understanding Lawrence Kubie's thesis set forth in his 1962 *Daedalus* piece, which we have referenced in footnote 29, above. As matured and reflective sports fanatics will concede, "erotic" refers not only to explicitly sexual behavior, but to notions of power to dominate, and submission to power, and, more generally, to ideas associated with sense-perception, as opposed to ideas associated with cognition. This underlies certain more readily recognized connections which come to the surface in forms of sexual abuse, such as rape, sodomy, intra-family violence, or simply the forms of psychosexual impotence in which the sex-act is performed with little more

oped quality of agapic emotion, that the thinker is able, willfully, to summon the creative cognitive powers needed to address a challenge.

The kind of deductive reductionism typical of Aristotelean formalism, is erotic, and hatefully anti-agapic, in type, as the psychopathological case of Kant and his philosophical writings, typifies the pathology of personal character inhering in the true follower of Aristotle's philosophy and method. Thus, Friedrich Schiller and his follower Wilhelm von Humboldt, set forth as the primary objective of a Classical-humanist form of education, the fostering of the development of the personal character of the future adult citizen; the efficient principle referenced by Schiller and Humboldt on this account, is rooted in the argument of *I Corinthians* 13, and it is also the underlying character of Plato's dialogues taken as a whole.

Hypothesis, and higher hypothesis, are each a special kind of object, an object of the form which Plato associates with the *good.* To introduce this conception, consider, first, the example offered by a very ordinary sort of theorem-lattice, as we defined this earlier, here.

In the simple theorem-lattice, the derivation of theorems has a certain ordering, in the sense that some theorems, once proven, serve as the basis for deriving later theorems. This sense of ordering implies ordering *in*

time. Nonetheless, the hypothesis underlying that lattice undergoes no modification during the time a sequence of theorems unfolds: from beginning, through to the end, the hypothesis remains unchanged; it is the veritable "alpha and omega" of that theorem-lattice. In Plato's method, every hypothesis, including every higher hypothesis, has this same property: it is the unchanging "alpha and omega" of whatever process of lattice-generation it underlies. In all, higher hypothesis is subsumed by God, the unsurpassable "hypothesis," the ultimate *Good.* Yet, every *relatively valid* hypothesis also imitates that form, as a lesser *good.*[37]

Agapē is the motivating state of mind which corresponds to the experience of any valid, or relatively valid such *good.*

Every person engaged in cognitive concentration, has lived through a relevant experiment: One's mind is working on the problem, up to the point the concentration collapses, as it were a man who suddenly toppled over, and fell asleep during a brisk walk. This might occur when one were exhausted, but we are considering only the type of case in which exhaustion was not determining. The motivation for the cognitive concentration has collapsed, as if the current had suddenly been cut off from an electronic device, as if the "batteries had died." Consider the instance, in which taking a break to participate in working through, or hearing a good performance of J.S. Bach, Haydn, Mozart, Beethoven, Schubert, or Brahms, returns one to one's cognitive undertaking with full powers of concentration restored—"batteries fully recharged." From this vantage-point, we turn our attention to certain identical features of Classical art-forms and valid axiomatic-revolutionary discoveries of physical principle. We are considering a topic which might be entitled: *cognitive energy.*

In Classical art-forms, the place of a mathematical discontinuity is taken by the ultimate expression of ambiguity, *metaphor.* During his 1948-1952 project, to refute Wiener's absurd claim, that human communication could be represented by statistical "information theory," the present author adopted the policy, that, although the case against Wiener could be made best from the standpoint of technological progress's increasing the productive powers of labor, it would be necessary to show that what was true for physical science,

---

than a "sex-as-power," animalist pleasure-seeking impulse, for domination or submission. In the instance of the "Don Juan," or "Macho" type, this may be expressed as a person who is either emotionally confused by, or even virtually incapable of, a human quality of enduring attachment to merely one woman. "Macho" Don Juan protests, with all the feigned sincerity of indignation such an inveterate confidence man might muster, "Me psycho-sexually impotent?: you have to be kidding!" In healthy states, the "erotic" impulse (*eros*) is associated with ideas within the domain of sense-perception; whereas, all ideas associated with cognition are associated with the emotional impulse of *agapē* The neurotically pathological characteristic of philosophical empiricism, neo-Kantian romanticism, and positivism, is typified in the extreme by the sexual history of such empiricists as Francis Bacon, Thomas Hobbes, and Jeremy Bentham. These three typify the neurotically confused state of mind essential to such philosophical currents. All of the ideas which are distinctively characteristic of Plato and of Christianity are within the domain of *agapē,* as *I Corinthians* 13 denies the quality of "Christian" to any ostensibly worthy act, which is not generated and controlled by *agapē.* Thus, the "Macho" type of neurotic responds to that challenge to his beliefs which is beyond what he senses he might be able to refute, not with reason, but with outbursts of an erotic quality of screaming, shouting, fist-waving rage. The "neurotic distortion of the creative process" which occupied Kubie's attention, is the result of the inappropriateness of the summoning of the erotic quality of emotional impulse, to address a challenge which requires the kind of ideas summonable only by the agapic impulse pecular to Platonic ideas.

---

37. This definition of the *good,* is congruent with Leibniz's definitions for the *monad.* See, notably, *Monadology,* 9-18, pp. 149-150 [footnote 1].

was also true for the generation and transmission of knowledge in Classical art-forms.

Thus, the study of "information" from the standpoint of technological progress, was parallelled by focus upon three closely related forms of non-plastic Classical media: poetry, drama, and the Classical art-song, the latter centered upon the Classical German *lied,* of Mozart, Beethoven, Schubert, Schumann, and Brahms, all compared with the Romantic *lied* of Hugo Wolf and Richard Strauss.

The standpoint in music, from which Classical forms of drama, poetry, and song were examined during that time, was the principle of motivic thorough-composition, as typified by Wolfgang Mozart's K.475 product of his study of the Bach *Musical Offering,* and the influence of that, and closely related Mozart compositions in later Classical composition. Today, the present author would have written of that approach, that keys and modes are hypotheses underlying the theorem-lattices of Classical forms of musical compositions, and that motivic thorough-composition, as typified by the Mozart K.475, is a prototype for higher hypothesis as the subject of musical composition.[38]

Thus, effective Classical musical composition, especially since those aspects of the work of J.S. Bach so deeply admired and emulated by Mozart, Beethoven, *et al.,* is an exercise in *agapē.* Similarly, Classical tragedy, and great Classical poetry, which rely upon the implicit *bel-canto* well-tempering of the well-spoken language, as the medium for speech, embody the developmental principle of the Greek Classical tragedy and Socratic dialogue. This is that cognitive medium of artistic development, which such poetry and drama employ, to instruct musical composition in the principles of musical dialogue, called polyphony, the which is the principle of Classical artistic development.

It is those artistic resolutions of ambiguity which carry the mind from one hypothesis to another, whether in poetry, drama, music, or plastic art-forms, which are the principle of change underlying Classical forms of artistic composition. This is that principle of Reason in art, which the psychosexually impotent Immanuel Kant could not recognize.[39] Those ambiguities which can not be resolved (e.g., "explained") deductively, as mere simile, symbolism, or hyperbole, are metaphors. These metaphors, which exist implicitly in the subjunctive mood, are the *Geistesmassen* of art.[40] Hence, during the

---

38. A few points of clarification must be supplied here, respecting the stages of the development, and related indebtednesses, of the author's progress to his present views on the subject of music. First, although the author's knowledge of lattice principles dates from his study of the work of Harvard's George David Birkhoff, during the late 1940's, he did not employ the theorem-lattice as a pedagogical approach to the principle of hypothesis until a middle 1950's manuscript examining problems of Operations Research from the standpoint of economic principles. In a sense, the author's views on motivic thorough-composition had perhaps a greater role in prompting the author to employ the pedagogy of theorem-lattices, than the other way around. By 1952, the author's views on motivic thorough-composition, were centered upon the traceable influence of Mozart's K.475 on Beethoven, Brahms, *et al.* This is typified by such matters, as the recognition of Brahms' direct quotation from this Bach-Mozart source in the C-minor (First) Symphony, and the direct quotation from the *Adagio Sostenuto* (measures 70-85) of Beethoven's Opus 106, as the motivic germ opening Brahms' Fourth (E-minor) Symphony (measures 2-19). During the same interval, 1948-1952, the author had chosen the characteristics of the composition of the German Classical *lied,* from Mozart through Brahms, as the key to all music, including all Classical instrumental compositions, and had emphasized the origins of music in the singing of ancient Classical poetry, and related principles of irony in Classical drama, especially Classicial tragedy. The next qualitative advance, as contrasted to gradual ones, came through collaboration with immediate associates and others, the others including, most emphatically, his dear friend, Professor Norbert Brainin, former Primarius of the Amadeus Quartet. In the first phase, 1979-1985, the emphasis was upon the implications of tuning from the standpoint of Florentine *bel canto* modes of voice-training. During that period, beginning 1981, the author projected the compilation of a text on the scientific principles underlying Classical musical composition, which became

Book I (On the Human Singing Voice) of *A Manual on the Rudiments of Tuning and Registration,* ed. by John Sigerson and Kathy Wolfe (Washington, D.C.: Schiller Institute, 1992). In the preparation of the forthcoming Book II (On the motivic thorough-composition and the ensemble), Professor Brainin outlined his own discovery of approximately two decades, respecting the relationship between Joseph Haydn's launching of *Motivführung* with his own Opus 33 quartets, and the revolution in motivic thorough-composition which Mozart launched, from approximately 1782-1783 onward, in response to Haydn's program (e.g., Mozart's six quartets dedicated to Haydn). See, Lyndon H. LaRouche, Jr., "Musical memory and thorough-composition," *Executive Intelligence Review,* Vol. 22, No. 35, Sept. 1, 1995, and the relevant addendum, "Norbert Brainin on Motivführung," *Executive Intelligence Review,* Vol. 22, No. 38, Sept. 22, 1995.

39. I.e., *Critique of Judgment.*

40. It is important to stress, that the subjunctive mood is not the grammatical forms with which its employment may, or may not be associated. The subjunctive mood is the mood of hypothesis, the mood of thought taking thought-processes as an object. Its Classical expression is the relevant literature of Greece, such as the Homeric epics, the great tragedies of Athens' Golden Age, and the dialogues of Plato. The type of Classical Greek literature which presents the actuality of the subjunctive mood (as distinct from a mere accident of conventions in grammatical forms) is a trio, of persons from two cities of different cultural heritage, interacting in a common setting, with one or more representatives of the pagan gods of Olympus. The actual events are shared in common, but those propositions, generated in response to the events, lead to theorems which are, respectively, mutually inconsistent. One character's, or the audience's, comparison of the differing mental pro-

course of the 1948-1952 study, the present author employed this sense of "metaphor" to embrace the expression of Platonic hypothesis in both physical science and Classical art-forms.

All successful art meeting those standards, evokes the same sense of uplifting agapic beauty we experience otherwise in those activities of the individual mind, through which original, or reenacted, valid, axiomatic-revolutionary discoveries of principle are generated. Such art is an integral part of science, in the broader sense of science. Such art increases the potential productive powers of labor, in the same sense that technological progress does. Such art also "recharges the batteries" of the individual's, and society's exercise of its creative powers of reason.

All too often, in observing discussions of mathematical, or of scientific work, we may be startled to recognize that the discussion we are witnessing, is painted in fresh coats of gray upon gray, proceeding with the implied assumption, that there is no emotional motivation in scientific thought as such, but only in arguments about its conclusions. Poor actor Leonard Nimoy, trapped for eternity in endless sequels of "Star Trek," babbling forever the idiot-savant's: *true scientific "logic" is a quality free from emotions*!

John Keats' *Ode on a Grecian Urn* spoke elegantly for Plato: truth is beauty, and beauty is truth. It is the passion of a mind gripped by a prescience of great beauty, which impels the creative thinker to ascend the impossible alp of scientific risks. Well-meaning laymen speak, foolishly, of financial rewards as motives for scientific (or, artistic) work. Feed a scientist, nourish his family, and offer him the opportunity to meet the kind of challenge which inspires him; freed of distracting such matters, his incentive is his passion never to lose that sense of a (Leibnizian) pursuit of happiness, the which is for him, or her, the lure of the scientific (like the Classical artistic) profession. The sense of truth is the source of the sense of overwhelming beauty; the recall of the emotion one associates with that sense of beauty, is the passion which drives one to push forward, one more step, and another, in pursuit of truth. Like Edmund Hillary, the scientist climbs the Everest of science—and Classical art, "because it is there." Keats' *Ode* is dedicated, passionately, to the triumph of *agapē*

over *eros*.[41]

Such is "cognitive energy." The composition and performance of the Classical art-form are the mirror-image of valid scientific discovery, on this account. Thus, does art command the power to "recharge the batteries" of the cognitive process for the scientist. That is a subject which, however curious that might seem, at first hearing, belongs to the department of economics: to the Leibnizian science of *physical economy.*

It is relevant here, to consider what might be described as a "structured" feature to *agapē,* a feature presented in the clearest way by considerations of technological attrition.

We have already indicated, that the Riemann topological series of hypotheses, typified, symbolically, by *(n+1)/n,* corresponds to a series of formal-mathematical discontinuities. Each such discontinuity corresponds to a corresponding singularity, an added "dimension" of the series of manifolds. All of the singularities functionally extant at the time each of the manifolds is in operation (subjectively and in corresponding practice), is efficiently present in every interval of thought-action of the person whose judgment and practice are being directed in accord with that manifold. Thus, we may apply the notion of implicitly enumerable densities of discontinuities, for any arbitrarily selected interval of thought-action, for that manifold's influence, under those general conditions.

---

41. In music, for example, the difference between a Classical and Romantic style of performance of a Classical composition (e.g., Mozart, Beethoven, Schubert, Schumann, Brahms) is implicit in conductor Wilhelm Furtwängler's instruction, to perform "between the notes." In the simplest degree, this requires that the performer express the counterpoint, rather than present a sensuous array of individual notes. To this end, the emphasis must be upon the motivic implications of the interval as an element of change, avoiding resort to erotic obsession with the utterance of the individual chord or note as such. Ultimately, it requires that each interval be performed with an eye to the hypothesis established by the concluding resolution of that developmental process which is the composition taken in its entirety. This applies not only to recognizing the proper relative tempi among movements, etc., as motivic considerations of the composition as a whole demand this; it prohibits decadently erotic emphasis upon uttering individual tones, in movements performed with exaggerated slowness for this purpose, and, on the contrary, excessive velocity, used to bury the meaninglessness of the performance under a sensuous heap of haste. It means a hatred of misrepresenting compositions through resort to readings of portions of a Classical score, such as Schumann, as "passage work" imported to make the composer appeal more erotically to the taste of a decadent Manhattan audience. The same applies to Classical drama and poetry. In good art, there is no symbolism, but, rather, the expression of interdependent empyreal ideas and agapic passions, expressed by metaphor.

---

cesses leading to the different reactions, and related ultimate outcomes, is the actuality of the subjunctive mood. Hence, the dialogues of Plato are all written in the subjunctive mood.

Cancel the British System, Save the People

The increase of the density of discontinuities, in such modes, has the twofold quality of "tension" and "potential." The "potential" corresponds to the relative increase of power over nature, *per capita* and *per* square kilometer of the planet's surface. The "tension" corresponds to a higher development of the internal (subjective) mental state of the relevant person. The increase in potential, corresponds to capacity for effectiveness of action; the increase of "tension," corresponds to an increase in the psychological motivation for action, to an increased sense of agapic, subjective "energy."[42]

The notion of hypothesis, and higher hypothesis, as of the timeless form of a *good,* defines these notions as what Kepler defined as *Reason,* and Leibniz as *necessary and sufficient reason.* A related term, to the same general effect, is *universal characteristics.* The significance of the latter term is shown more clearly from the standpoint of the present author's original discoveries in the domain of physical economy.

2. The 'LaRouche-Riemann Method'

There can be no competent teaching and practice of economics, which does not reject, and that absolutely, the entirety of the doctrine of "causality," as that doctrine has been passed down from Paolo Sarpi *et al.,* to the teaching of social theory and science, in virtually every classroom and textbook of secondary and higher education today. Physical science, as Leibniz applied this to economy,[43] demolishes, absolutely, two classes of conceptions of that Venetian tradition which is hegemonic in the economics classroom today. Physical economy overturns all widely taught doctrines of "profit" and "surplus value," by showing that the only possible origin of net growth and ("macroeconomic")

profitability, is the increase of the productive powers of labor, through investment in (principally) scientific and technological progress. Physical economy demolishes the ordinary notions of "causality," directly, by showing that present economic behavior is as much determined by the influence of the future upon today, as by the heritage of the recent and more remote past.[44]

The pivotal point of reference for addressing these two failures by omission, of virtually all taught economics today, is the general notion of the hypothesis as a *good,* referenced here, above. The fact that an hypothesis has the "timeless" quality referenced there, permits that hypothesis to act as the efficient agent of the future, upon the present. The difficulty is, as early as during the medium to long term, technological attrition gives us a future which is not determined by a single hypothesis, but, rather, by a series of hypotheses.[45] Thus, the required hypothesis for determining the future outcome of present choices is that higher hypothesis, which subsumes the relevant sequence of hypotheses. On that account, no science of economics could be competent, were it not premised upon Leibniz's principle of universal characteristics, the which is derived from Plato's method of hypothesis.

On the same premises, Riemann's principal work, fairly described as *mathematics defined from the standpoint of experimental physics,* provides an indispens-

---

42. This is not to be confused with erotic qualities of manic elation. The subjective effect is "calming," directly opposed to manic. The increased capacity for action, is associated, metaphorically, with the notion of serenity and a source of "energy" for action. It suggests the quality of serenity in that great military commander who has achieved the appropriate capacity for what Carl Philipp von Clausewitz references in use of the term *Entschlossenheit.*

43. Gottfried W. Leibniz, "Society and Economy" (1671), trans. by John Chambless, *Fidelio), Vol. 1, No. 3, Fall 1992. This is Leibniz's original work in physical economy, in which some among the most crucial principles of hiw own later work, and those of such American System followers as Alexander Hamilton, Mathew and Henry Carey, and Friedrich List, are already affirmed.*

44. This issue of the manner in which the future acts efficiently upon the present, has been an included topic of the present writer in a number of locations, in which the implications of musician Ramon Llull's use (*Ars Magna*) of Plato's principle of memory, has been addressed. Senior Operations Researcher Kenneth Arrow contributed remarks on this subject, to *Pragmatic Gradualism: Reform Strategy for Russia,* Valery Makarov, project director (Moscow: Economic Transition Group, Aug. 1995): "… No doubt many factors operate, but the one which I want to stress, the role of time, is intimately linked with a deeper understanding of the price system and markets. There is a future as well as a present in economic life… . What I mean by the role of time can be stated paradoxically: the future influences the present. This seems like a violation of our ordinary laws of causality, but what is really meant is that our expectations of the future will affect what we do in the present." (p. 42) See, also, Lyndon H. LaRouche, Jr., "Kenneth Arrow Runs Out of Ideas, But Not Words," *op. cit.,* and Lyndon H. LaRouche, Jr., "How Hobbes' Mathematics Misshaped Modern History," *Fidelio,* Vol. V, No. 1, Spring 1996. The same topic, directly referencing Arrow's referenced remarks cited here, was an included feature of a memorandum of May 4, 1996, on the work of U.S. contributors to *Pragmatic Gradualism,* submitted to relevant Russian academicians: *More 'Nobel Lies.'* See *EIR Special Report,* May 31, 1996, pp. 34-47.

45. This is illustrated most forcefully by the history of the function of technological attrition in modern warfare. The case of development in deployed combat aircraft, during the 1939-1945 interval, is exemplary.

able service in the advancement of the science of physical economy. Given, a series of hypotheses, ordered according to the standard of mankind's increasing power over the universe, *per capita* and *per* square kilometer of the Earth's surface, we have a corresponding series of curved surfaces, each coordinate with a relevant, *n*-fold, physical space-time manifold. The series of such surfaces corresponds to the functional impact of the relevant higher hypothesis, serving as the yardstick by means of which the future may determine the selection of choices in the present.

As extremely relevant as Riemann's discoveries are, the present author's discoveries in economics could not have been derived from the root of Riemann's work. The impulse for increase of man's power over nature, *per capita* and *per* square kilometer, is expressed implicitly by the notion of Riemannian potential arising from the pages of the 1854 habilitation dissertation. However, for his own discoveries, the present author's debt to the prompting by Leibniz, is more or less direct.

Riemann's notion of a succession of manifolds of increasing power, implies a potential, a potential which might be expressed in terms of increasing *cardinality*: increasing density of discontinuities for any arbitrarily chosen interval of human action. To account for the historical actuality of mankind's increase of potential relative population-density, an additional standard of measure, an additional notion of function, must be supplied.

That additional standard of measure was supplied by this author, during the 1948-1952 interval. The discovery was provoked by the shocking absurdity of Norbert Wiener's claim, that the characteristic distinctions of living processes and human behavior could be subsumed under Ludwig Boltzmann's theorem in statistical thermodynamics, the so-called H-theorem. Although Wiener appeared to adopt the standard of some leading biologists, and others, in noting that the formal distinction of living processes, was that they defied entropy, his attempt at a radical-positivist form of mechanistic explanation for living and human behavior, was disgusting. Since, the fact is, that living and human behavior are distinguished from putatively non-living processes by "not entropy," the absurdity of Wiener's arbitrary claims for his "information theory," obliged the present writer to focus upon the problem of supplying an alternate, sane definition for "negative entropy." Although the writer had not yet encountered Leibniz's *Society and Economy* at that time, the starting-point of his approach to refuting Wiener was that of a Leibniz student, broadly identical to that of Leibniz's 1671 paper.

Reduced to essentials, the writer's opening argument was this. The *per capita* productive potential of both the member of the labor-force, as an individual, and in the work-place, is an expression of investments, by society, in the development of both that person, and his work-place. This cumulative investment can be represented in terms of *per-capita,* and *per*-square-kilometer values of "market baskets" of consumption by households and the productive workplace and its essential environment. This functional notion of a relationship between productive potential, and the market-baskets of "investment" in developing and maintaining that productive potential, may be compared with the notion of "energy of the system," in classroom thermodynamics. Thus, by comparing the outputs and inputs of the population and its productive processes, including education and health as physical costs, the distinctions of "energy of the system" and "free energy" are implied.[46]

However, that was only the beginning. The characteristic of modern agro-industrial society, is technological attrition. The study of what is known of the physical economy, and associated demographics, of pre-historic and historic existence of society, prior to the Fifteenth-century rise of modern European civilization, exhibits the same principle, governing the rise and collapse of societies. The essential difference, is that modern European civilization has stepped up the rate of development (and technological attrition) greatly, far exceeding all earlier human experience. This development occurs at a cost, a cost measurable in terms of market baskets. In other words, the increase of the productive powers of labor occurs at a cost. That cost is, predominantly, the increase in *per-capita* and *per*-square-kilometer absolute (physical) cost of the "energy of the system," as expressed in market-basket terms.[47]

---

46. On this and the following paragraphs, see Lyndon H. LaRouche, Jr., *So, You Wish To Learn All About Economics?,* 2nd ed. (Washington, D.C: EIR News Service, 1995). Relevant statistics and other relevant supplementary material are to be found in *To Save The Nation* (Leesburg, Va.: LaRouche Exploratory Committee, 1995).

47. As a matter of accounting for the point of reference from which the author's work on this subject began: The observations identified in this, and the preceding paragraph, were the adopted starting-point, during 1948, for the author's rebuttal of Wiener's statistical dogma. The features of that starting-point bearing on the subjects of "negative entropy" and scientific method, were products of study, including the philosophical studies of the 1930's. The notions of what constituted "energy of the

This, and related considerations, leads to the following yardstick, expressed in terms of inequalities: *The requirement for the successful continuation of an economy is, that the ratio of "free energy" to "energy of the system," must not decline, despite the dependency of this ratio upon continuing increases of the absolute market-basket cost of "energy of the system," per capita and per square kilometer.*

Science As Art

The crucial features of the present writer's contributions to Leibniz's science of physical-economy, are four:

1. The development of the needed metric for a science of physical-economy: an appropriate conception of what should be signified, functionally, as a "not-entropic" increase of potential relative population-density;

2. The establishment of the appropriate notion of the characteristic function of economy as subjective, rather than objective. Economic processes as characteristically cognitive for purposes of defining physical-economic function. This is accomplished through a direct focus upon the principal irony of economic science, that a thought, in the form of a *Platonic idea* (valid discovery of principle), of imputably transinfinitesimal mass and velocity, is ostensibly the efficient, catalytic, cause for vast physical changes in man's relationship to the universe, *per capita* and *per* square kilometer of our planet's surface. The related notion, that all science is a Classical art-form, that poetry must supersede mathematics in science: that mathematics and experimental physical science are subsumed by a generalization of the notion of metaphor, as metaphor is the characteristic function within all Classical art-forms.

3. That the ultimate proof of the validity of the human cognitive process, is not the principle of "repeatable experiment," but, rather, the fact of mankind's increasing potential relative population-density, and correlated potential for improvement in demographic characteristics of individuals, households, and the population as a whole, through increase of the cardinality of human cognitive action. *The universe is manifestly predisposed, by design, to obedient submission to those valid, axiomatic-revolutionary discoveries of principle which are generated by the individual person's willful, cognitive processes of creative reason.*[48]

4. The significance, as we have shown, of Riemann's discovery, for providing the needed notions of measurement required to show the connection between scientific and physical-economic progress.

The addition of the fourth, to shape the application of the preceding three discoveries to empirical treatment of actual physical-economic processes, constitutes what has been known, since December 1978, as the *LaRouche-Riemann Method.*[49]

---

system" for a modern industrial economy, were premised largely on a combination of the personal experience, being apprenticed to factory work, and related activities, as preparation for a management consulting career, during non-school-time periods of his adolescence, and relevant experiences in Bengal during the early months of 1946. The notion of putting aside nominal prices, to regard the entirety of a national, or an international economy, as a network, in terms of the standpoint of bills of materials and process-sheets, was the basis for his training and practice in management consulting. The special distinctions of his approach to defining bills of materials and process sheets, was the including of technological progress, education, and health-care, as an integral part of the national cost of the local process of production.

48. This use of the term "design," respecting the disposition which our universe has acquired by design, is congruent with the notions of Leibniz's *Monadology*: *op. cit.,* 51-60, pp. 156-157. The highest Good, the ultimate hypothesis, the ultimate Monad, is the "alpha and omega" of all of the existence of the universe. Thus, the characteristic imbued in every theorem of the theorem-lattice defined by that hypothesis, reflects the future as hypothesis reflects all possible future states of its own theorem-lattice. Hence, the characteristic of the universe's response to relatively valid, axiomatic-revolutionary discoveries of principle, is the increase in man's relative power of dominion in the universe as a whole. The fright which explodes in the Aristotelean or empiricist, when any conception of this is presented, is illustrated, as Leibniz notes this fact, by the so-called "mortalist" doctrine of the soul, transmitted into the Sixteenth and Seventeenth centuries by the students of Pomponazzi. The argument of these "mortalists" is congruent with the tautological fallacy which Euler employs to attack Leibniz: the root, is the popularization of that absurd representation of "infinity" inhering in the method of Aristotle. A wag might say, on this account, that "all followers of Aristotle are schlemiels."

49. In consequence of an argument, between this writer's circles, and some of Dr. Edward Teller's talented friends at Lawrence Livermore Laboratories, on the matter of isentropic compression in ignition of fusion processes, the writer proposed to show that Riemann's principle of isentropic compression, as typified by Riemann's *Fortpflanzung* paper, had a general application, including its role in presenting the best economic forecasting tool for computer-assisted forecasts. The author reduced the principled features of his work in economics to the relevant sets of inequalities and constraints required for a computer "modelling," treating the Riemann-like, technology-driven phase-shifts in economic processes as the basis for showing the characteristics of current economic trends. This produced a series of quarterly forecasts for the U.S. economy, which were continued by the weekly *Executive Intelligence*

Although this method makes use of mathematics and physical science, it is essentially the treatment of mathematics and physical science as subsumed features of a Classical art-form, the defining, subsuming characteristic of which, is the equivalence of metaphor to the primary features of human cognitive activity. In that sense, we are obliged to speak of "art as science."

Before we proceed to focus the camera of the mind upon the argument underlying each of the four topics just listed, let us clear the scene (so to speak) of some of that distracting bric-a-brac, whose presence, today, usually prevents students, key government officials and other policy-shapers, and others, from focussing rationally upon the crisis-problems of today's planet.

To be a competent economist today, one must have a taste for Classical stylists of a Platonic disposition and wit, in the footsteps, for example, of a François Rabelais, or Jonathan Swift. To clear one's mind to think with scientific rigor, one must be capable of seeing that the pompous verities of the privileged and popular of one's own time, and earlier, too, are ridiculous pretenses. Like Swift's Gulliver, one might think of one's self as some poor lout, who is nonetheless a veritable titan amid the royal, lordly, and lackey pygmies around him, or might fancy a view of early Eighteenth-century England, as a pack of witless, ever-rutting Yahoos, being herded and culled by what appears to be a lordly pack of horses' rears. We could not, in good conscience, be so tolerant as Swift was, to the economists, sociologists, psychologists, and, lowest of all, popular journalists, who pollute the prevailing sentimentality of our own times. Considering such creatures as those professionals of today, a man, beset by packs of such misanthropes, must be forgiven, if he imagines, in the odd moment, that he might be a modern Gulliver, the only man with a functioning watch on a planet full of cannibals.

Those allusions to Rabelais and Swift might be misjudged, as spoken lightly; but, they are in dead earnest, and do not exaggerate the enormity of the problem confronting the world today. Consider what man is, in contrast to what the debased opinion of today's empiricists

presumes man to be. Then, it should be clear, that we have perpetrated no libel in speaking so contemptuously of those vastly overpopulated social-theoretical professions, the which have turned our universities into refuse dumps for dead minds and rotting morals.

The rise of the Enlightenment's influence, during the course of the Seventeenth through Nineteenth centuries, witnessed the spread of those mental illnesses in the forms of empiricism and Cartesianism, and, later, as Kantianism. Each nation, today, has a heritage of the most radical extremes of such axiomatic misassumptions, respecting the nature of man: For England, for example, Thomas Hobbes, John Locke, and Bernard Mandeville; for France, the neo-Cartesian positivists and their bastard intellectual progeny, the existentialists; for Germany, the neo-Kantians and existentialists; for the U.S., our pragmatists; and, so on. Influences of that ilk are paramount in our universities, in the educational programs of public education, and, colored with pornographic, day-glo hues, as the commonplace truisms reigning within the common, back-fence variety of gossip, everywhere.

This same immorality, spreading out of those cesspools which are our universities' departments of sociology, psychology, anthropology, political science, philosophy, modern language, and history, is the characteristic feature of the editorial practice of our leading news and entertainment media. It is the foundation for the filthiest concoctions of gossip, used as weapons of political influence, as by both leading press and corrupt prosecutors. English and French "social science," has transformed the majority of the hegemonic currents among ostensibly educated U.S. citizens, their children, and others, into "Yahoos." It is a mark of the times, that "Yahoo" is an irony of incontestable appropriateness, to describe those citizens who profess themselves to be the "single-issue minded" Torquemadas of the public conscience.

This moral rot may be summed up, fairly, as deeply embedded, axiomatic acceptance of that notion, which the British empiricists define as "human nature." The overlapping, paradigmatic figures of common reference for this social doctrine, include Francis Bacon, John Locke, Bernard de Mandeville, François Quesnay, Giammaria Ortes, David Hume, Adam Smith, Jeremy Bentham, James and John Stuart Mill, and the American pragmatists. They include the followers of Bertrand Russell; the Frankfurt School of Theodor Adorno, Hannah Arendt, *et al.*; the German existentialists, in-

---

Review (EIR) into the close of 1983. These, described since late 1978 as "The LaRouche-Riemann Method," were the only successful forecasts of the 1979-1983 interval. They were discontinued only when *EIR* caught the U.S. government and Federal Reserve System introducing, abruptly, such wild fakery of reported data, during the closing months of 1983, that no rational forecast dependent on official data was possible any longer.

cluding the proto-Nazi Friedrich Nietzsche, and Nazi official Martin Heidegger; Jean-Paul Sartre, *et al.*; the institutions associated with Dr. Kurt Lewin, and with such Tavistock Centre creatures as Sigmund Freud (a.k.a. "Sigmoid Fraud"), Dr. John Rawlings Rees, Melanie Klein, and that serial killer of coal miners, Dr. Eric Trist.

These varieties of nasty creatures differ only as do sundry specimens of disease-bearing lice. Their commonality is seen most clearly, in the light of physical-economy: The Malthusian economic dogmas of François Quesnay, Giammaria Ortes, Adam Smith, Jeremy Bentham, and the Nineteenth-century utilitarians, reflect that commonality in the clearest terms of experimental reference. The most shameless expression, until Adolf Hitler, of the principle of evil common to all these lice, putative economists and others, is the late Friedrich von Hayek's choice, the satanic Bernard de Mandeville, he the spiritual progenitor of the fascistic Mont Pelerin Society. The essence of this evil, is expressed in the economic domain, as the Locke-Mandeville-Quesnay dogma of "free trade," or, in the original Quesnay French, *laissez-faire.* Throughout what is called "European culture," there is no morally abominable feature of economic doctrine, social theory, or mathematical physics, which is not rooted in the equivalence of the Mandeville-Quesnay dogma of "free trade" to that Newton-Clarke-Euler dogma of "infinite series," which Euler employed for his tautologically fallacious fraud of 1761, against Leibniz.[50]

Sometimes, it appears, that people accept the *laissez faire* dogmas of the evil Quesnay and Adam Smith, because they have been brainwashed into accepting the influence of Newton, Euler, *et al.* respecting axiomatics of mathematical physics. Admittedly, the substitution of the virtual reality of "infinite series" for real-world physics, prescribes that economic processes be treated from the standpoint of Hobbes' principles, which underlie the statistical gas theory of Lord Rayleigh and Ludwig Boltzmann. On the other hand, sometimes it appears, that it is empiricist social theory which prejudices the mind to accept the notions of causality and infinite series of the empiricists. Obviously, the doctrine of social behavior promulgated by Hobbes, prescribes that mankind's experience in the domain of sense-perception, be premised upon a notion of "random walk" through a ki-

nematic manifold. One who wishes, passionately, to defend such a mechanistic world-outlook, must fear Gottfried Leibniz, must be disposed to lie ferociously about Leibniz, and to seek to discredit him in every way an hysterical gossip might contrive, even if that means going to bed with a certain bachelor, Dr. Samuel Clarke's lunatic client, Isaac Newton.[51]

The principle of evil inhering in Hobbes, François Quesnay, and Adam Smith, is presented in its most naked terms by Bernard Mandeville.[52] The form in

---

51. Isaac Newton's apotheosis as the "English Descartes," was arranged by the Paris-based control agent of Venice's intelligence service, the Abbot Antonio Conti (1677-1749). Dr. Samuel Clarke was a leader in an English circle run by Conti, and was Conti's controller of Newton during the period of the Leibniz-Clarke-Newton correspondence. The setting for Conti's apotheosis of the unfortunate Newton, was the implications of England's 1701 Act of Settlement, which, for a time, designated Leibniz's patroness, Electress Sophie of Hanover, as heir to the throne. Leibniz, then the most powerful intellect in Europe, with a powerful, international network under his leadership, and the most deadly enemy of the Venice's special interest, loomed, until Sophie's death in 1714, as the prospective Prime Minister of England. Conti picked up poor looney Isaac Newton to serve as a cat's paw, in Venice's desperate concern to discredit that Leibniz, who soon emerged as the philosophical progenitor of the American Revolution, its Declaration of Independence, and the Preamble of its Federal Constitution. [*Cf.* H. Graham Lowry, *How The Nation Was Won,* Vol. I (Washington, D.C.: Executive Intelligence Review, 1987).] On the subject of Newton's scientific work, the following, as reported in "How Bertrand Russell Became an Evil Man," *Fidelio,* Vol. III, No. 3, Fall 1994, Note 234, p. 59. The monetary theorist John Maynard Keynes was entrusted with the assessment of a chest of Isaac Newton's private scientific papers. Keynes, opening the chest, was shocked to find the scribblings of a superstitious lunatic, a Newton whom he described, in his report, as "the last of the magicians, the last of the Babylonians and Sumerians ... wholly devoid of scientific value"; see "Newton the Man," in *Newton Tercentenary Celebration* (Cambridge: Cambridge University Press, 1947). pp. 27-34.

52. Adam Smith was, beginning no later than 1763, an agent of the notorious William Petty (Fitzmaurice), Second Earl of Shelburne, best known as "Lord Shelburne," one-time Prime Minister of Britain, key representative of the British East India Company interest, and of Barings bank, and paymaster for the bribes employed to control the British Parliament of William Pitt the Younger. Shelburne was, also, the patron of the Jeremy Bentham who headed up the British foreign service, from 1782 on, and of the pack of creatures who passed for economists at the British East India Company's Haileybury School. Smith was assigned, in 1763, to assist a Shelburne project aimed both at undermining the economy of France, and destroying the independence of the English colonies in North America. To the latter end, Shelburne dispatched Smith to France, where he studied the works of Quesnay and other Physiocrats, whom he parodied and plagiarized for the production of his own anti-American tract, his 1776 *Wealth of Nations.* The evil in Smith may have resonated with that of Quesnay, but was firmly established earlier, in his 1759 *Theory of the Moral Sentiments,* the core of which is pure Mandeville. The relevant passage of the latter work most often cited by the present author, runs as follows. "... To man is allotted a much humbler department ... more suitable to the weakness of his

---

50. The sociological root of the doctrine of "linearization in the very small."

which this principle of evil is presented, is that Hobbes model which is otherwise the general plan for statistical gas theory, and for the use of infinite series as a substitute for physics. The argument is, that unless we wish to adopt Hobbes' alternative, the Divine Right of an Absolute Monarch to do as he might will, we must be content with a form of "libertarianism," a "social contract" derived from John Locke's defense of chattel slavery: "Life, Liberty, and Property," the Locke argument against which both the American War of Independence, and the war against the Confederacy were fought. Evil is, "Anything might be allowable, if it does not interfere with the superior, unchecked right of the property-owner." From the conception of "my body," "my family rights," "my personal sensitivities," and so on, as Lockean forms of "property," any evil done in the name of libertarianism might flow. From this is derived the anti-Christian ethics professed publicly by U.S. Supreme Court Associate Justice Antonin Scalia, that upon the "perfect democracy" of Lockean chaos, law may impose only those rules which are set, as guidelines, by the most recent caprices of majority opinion.

Every branch of social theory taught in leading unversities today, differs from every other branch as one cut of the same cloth might differ from another. All are but varieties of apologetics for this same moral and intellectual pollution exemplified by liberal economic dogma.

Under the influence of these and kindred misconceptions of "freedom" and its limits, during the past thirty-odd years, we have nearly destroyed what had been an admittedly imperfect, but successfully progressing civilization. Until changes in "cultural paradigms," induced during the mid-1960's and following, the modern sovereign nation-state republic had been premised upon promoting the benefits, implicitly to all, of investment in scientific and technological progress. During the recent thirty years, the damages which have been done to the mind, have been worse than that which has been done to their bodies. We must console the Lemuel Gulliver condemned to describing that Hellhole which our civilization is becoming.

Potential Relative Population-Density

That cause for our recalling Swift, is typified by viewing the moral degeneracy of those who fancy real-life economy as an "n-person, zero-sum game" out of the virtual reality of Von Neumann's and Morgenstern's theory of games.[53] This brings us to consider the first of the present author's four crucial contributions to Leibniz's science of physical economy, the notion of *potential relative population-density.*[54]

The distinguishing characteristic of the existence of the human species, is the increase of its population over that of any actual, or imaginably comparable type of higher ape. For the conditions which have existed on this planet during the recent two millions or so years, such a higher ape could not have exceeded a population of several millions, world wide. By the close of the medieval period of European history, circa A.D. 1439-1461,[55] the world's human population had attained several hundreds millions; from that point on, the impact

---

powers, and the narrowness of his comprehension; the care of his own happiness, of that of his family, his friends, his country.... [T]hough we are ... endowed with a very strong desire of those ends, it has been entrusted to the slow and uncertain determinations of our reason to find out the proper means of bringing them about. *Nature has directed us to the greater part of these by original and immediate instincts. Hunger, thirst, the passion which unites the two sexes, the love of pleasure, and the dread of pain, prompt us to apply those means for their own sakes, and without any consideration of their tendency to those beneficent ends which the great Director of nature intended to produce by them.* [emphasis added—LHL] The libertarian's immorality of Mandeville is clearly reflected in that passage from Smith, just as Smith's plagiarizing Quesnay's *laissez faire* is the basis for his own "free trade," and "Invisible Hand." Mandeville insists that even evil impulses of individuals are part of the process of interactions which leads to ultimate good, just as the evil Professor Milton Friedman argued in such locations as his April 16, 1980 TV interview on the *Phil Donahue Show.* On Mandeville, see H. Graham Lowry, *op. cit., passim.* Also, H. Graham Lowry, "The Mandeville Model," *Fidelio,* Vol. V, No. 1, Spring 1996.

53. John Von Neumann and Oskar Morgenstern, *Theory of Games and Economic Behavior,* 3rd ed. (Princeton: Princeton University Press, 1953). As those authors note [Note 1, page 1], the genesis of their book is found in a 1928 paper of Von Neumann, *Zur Theorie der Gesellschaftsspiele.* By 1938, Bertrand Russell devotee Von Neumann had committed himself publicly to the lunatic doctrine, that economic processes could be reduced to solutions to a set of linear inequalities. Together with another Bertrand Russell clone, Norbert Wiener, the modern dogmas of "cybernetics" and "systems analysis" were hewn into the form, as policies, they have dominated post-World War II practice.

54. On the practical representation of *potential relative population-density,* see Lyndon H. LaRouche, Jr., *So, You Wish to Learn All About Economics?, op. cit.* There are also editions in Spanish, Russian, Ukrainian, Polish, Armenian, and Georgian and Chinese editions in progress to print.

55. The interval, from the opening of the great ecumenical Council at Florence, to the accession of France's King Louis XI to establish the first modern sovereign nation-state republic. This period corresponds to the core of what is called the "Renaissance," e.g., the *Golden Renaissance,* as opposed to the Sixteenth-century emergence of the Venice-orchestrated *anti-Renaissance,* which came to be known as the *Enlightenment.* The conflict within European culture, to which we have been referring throughout this present paper, is efficiently, and accurately identified as the irreconcilable conflict of principle between the Renaissance and the Enlightenment.

Growth of European Population, Population-density, and Life-expectancy at Birth, Estimated for 100,000 B.C.-A.D. 1975

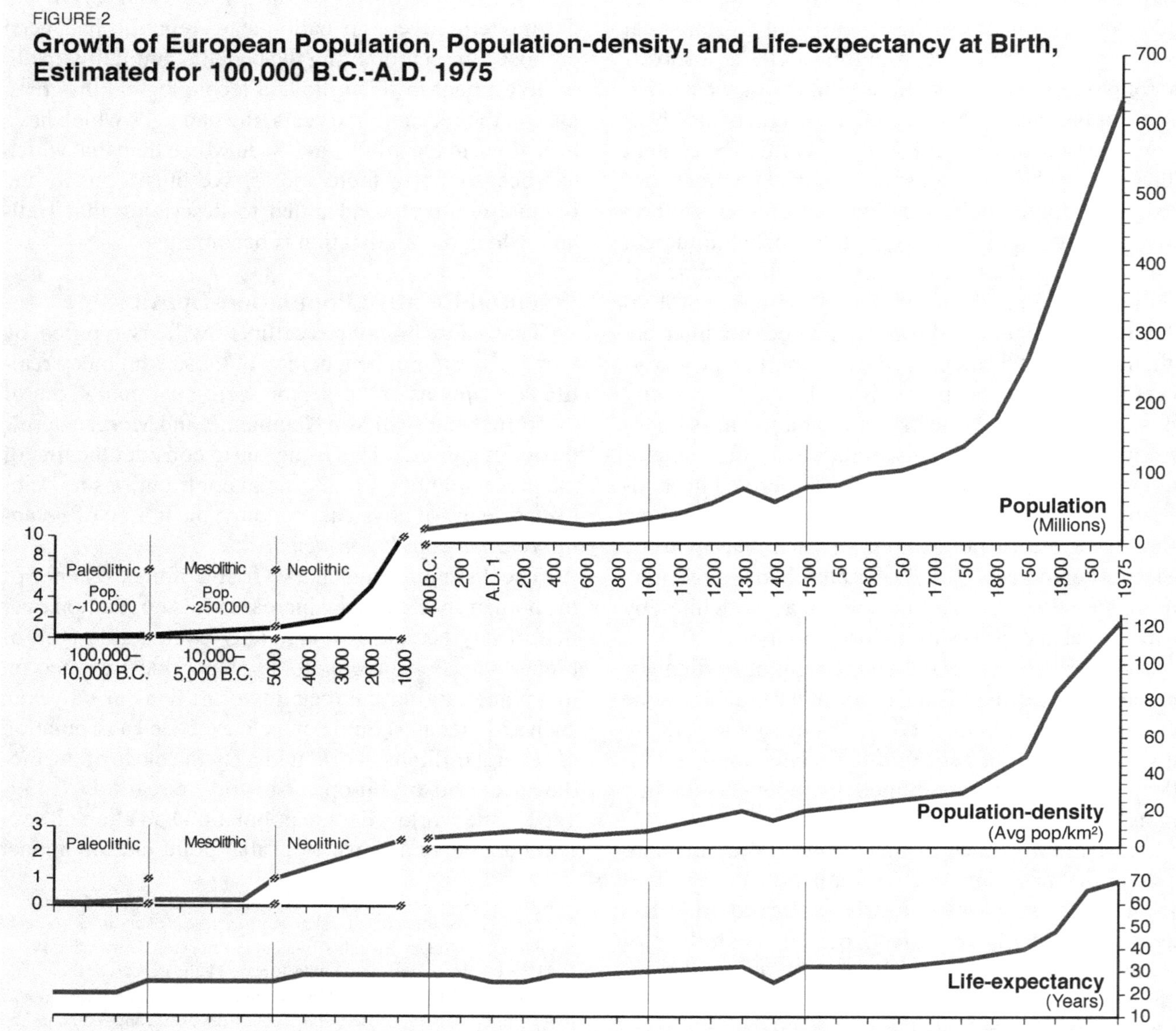

All charts are based on standard estimates compiled by existing schools of demography. None claim any more precision than the indicative; however, the scaling flattens out what might otherwise be locally, or even temporally, significant variation, reducing all thereby to the set of changes which is significant, independent of the quality of estimates and scaling of the graphs. Sources: For population and population-density, Colin McEvedy and Richard Jones, Atlas of World Population History, for life-expectancy, various studies in historical demography.

Note breaks and changes in scales.

of the combined development, in Europe, of modern scientific progress and the emergence of the modern sovereign nation-state,[56] has prompted a hyperbolic

56. Under feudalism, there was the notion of "nationality," but there were no nation-states. Rather, from the bowels of Babylon until the middle of the Fourteenth century, the civilization of the Mediterranean littoral, and immediately adjacent territories, was under the rule of *imperial law*. [See, Friedrich August Freiherr von der Heydte, *Die Ge-*

burtsstunde des Souveraenen Staates (Regensburg: Josef Habbel, 1952).] The land and the people were the property of an emperor, under which overlords, lords, and others, ruled over those territories and persons which had been parcelled out to them. From Babylon, through Rome and Byzantium, through Venice-dominated Fourteenth-century Europe, over ninety-five percent of the population of this planet, in every quarter, lived as virtual human cattle, or worse, under the rule of a form of rule by quasi-immortal oligarchical families, an oligarchy apotheosized as the pagan gods of Olympus. The idea of a modern Euro-

population-growth world-wide, to in excess of an estimated 5.2 billions presently [See **Figure 2**].

This is not limited to an increase in raw population. There is a correlated trend for improvement in demographic characteristics of total populations and their component cohorts. The combined trends are correlated with increase of both the consumption and production of essential market-basket components of both input and output, as measured *per capita, per* household, and *per* square kilometer of relevant land-area. These components include such physical components as agricultural and manufactured products, and improvements in land, and other infrastructural development of the occupied territories of the society. These include such elements of "soft" infrastructure as education and health-care [See **Table I**].

In light of the dependency of productivity upon both the development of the individual member of society, and of both the work-places and of infrastructure generally, one may readily discern a fact, which may be established with great rigor. The increase of the productive powers of labor, as measured in market-basket contents, *per capita, per* household, and *per* square kilometer of land-area, depends upon increase in the content of the relevant market-baskets of consumption. Relevant to the argument of Von Neumann, to increase the output of society, *per capita,* we must increase the input of society, *per capita.* Thus, summed up in terms of inequalities: *The successful growth of potential relative population-density, requires that the ratio of "free energy" to "energy of the system" not decrease, under the condition that this can not occur without an increase of the density of "energy of the system."*

Contrast this with the twofold absurdity of axiomatic presumptions, which underlie, inextricably, the foolish "zero-sum game" of Von Neumann's and Morgenstern's text. That is to say, consider, on one side, the absurdity of Von Neumann's and Morgenstern's axiom-

atic assumptions, as this pertains to the facts of physical economy. At the same time, consider the lunacy of Von Neumann's and Morgenstern's presumption, that prices, as treated in their games, represent functional measures of economic performance of societies considered in their entirety. Consider in that light, the sheer lunacy of the manner in which the modern economics classroom popularizes its mythical distinction between "micro-economics" and "macro-economics."

Like Wiener's statistical information theory, Von Neumann's systems analysis apotheosizes the worst banalities of radical logical positivism: Hobbes and Mandeville are taken to their radical extremes. Von Neumann, Hobbes, and Mandeville portray a linearized parody of actual man, and this in the very small; the result is elaborated, by simple extrapolation, all in an idiot-savant child's multi-dimensional parody of Euclidean space-time. There are no physical values, no physical realities in the virtual reality of Von Neumann's universe. There is only a fantastic montage: the Cheshire cat's grin of Jansci ("Johnny") Von Neumann, as an imaginary child, and the ring of the candy-store cash register.

All of the arguments, to the effect that a money-price ought to represent the action of a competitive market to arrive, asymptotically, at a level corresponding to the dogmatics of "marginal utility," are patently absurd, both by definition, and in light of facts of economic history of price movements. The "free trader's" argument is essentially that of Hobbes, Mandeville, Quesnay, *et al.*: That, it is the random interaction of the microeconomic events, aggregately under the statistical governance of the "Invisible Hand"—might one say, "ergodic process," which reveals what Adam Smith's "great Director of nature intended to produce" by these relatively blind, statistical interactions. That is, with some qualifications on tertiary points, the argument of Von Neumann and all among those who follow him in this matter.

In reality, throughout economic history, relative values of money prices are rigged. In some instances, the prices are set by decree; usually, prices are rigged by the action of monopolistic or oligopolistic financial powers; in the optimal circumstances, movements in relative price-levels among commodities are controlled indirectly, through the setting of the rules of the market-game, as by governments, or agreements among governments; in worse times, these powers are usurped by private financier cabals, such as those centered around

Development of Human Population, from Recent Research Estimates

	Life expectancy at birth (years)		Population density (per km2)	Comments	World population (millions)
Primate Comparison					
Gorilla			1/km2		.07
Chimpanzee			3-4/km2		1+
Man					
Australopithecines B.C. 4,000,000-1,000,000	14-15		1/ 10 km2	68% die by age 14	.07-1
Homo Erectus B.C. 900,000-400,000	14-15				1.7
Paleolithic (hunter-gatherers) B.C. 100,000-15,000	18-20+		1/ 10 km2	55% die by age 14; average age 23	
Mesolithic (proto-agricultural) B.C. 15,000-5,000	20-27				4
Neolithic, B.C. 10,000-3,000	25		1/km2	"Agricultural revolution"	10
Bronze Age B.C. 3,000-1,000	28		10/km2	50% die by age 14 Village dry-farming, Baluchistan, 5,000 B.C.: 9.61/km2 Development of cities: Sumer, 2000 B.C.: 19.16/km2 Early Bronze Age: Aegean, 3,000 B.C.: 7.5-13.8/km2 Late Bronze Age: Aegean, 1,000 B.C.: 12.4-31.3/km2 Shang Dynasty China, 1000 B.C.: 5/km2	50
Iron Age, B.C. 1,000-	28				50

Mediterranean Classical Period B.C. 500-A.D. 500	25-28		15+/km2	Classical Greece, Peloponnese: 35/km2
				Roman Empire:
				  Greece: 11/km2 Italy: 24/km2
				  Asia: 30/km2 Egypt: 179/km2*
				Han Dynasty China, B.C. 200-A.D. 200: 19.27/km2
				  Shanxi: 28/km2 Shaanxi: 24/km2
				  Henan: 97/km2* Shandong: 118/km2*
				* Irrigated river-valley intensive agriculture
					100-190

European Medieval Period A.D. 800-1300	30+		20+/km2	40% die by age 14 Italy, 1200: 24/km2 Italy, 1340: 34/km2 Tuscany, 1340: 85/km2 Brabant, 1374: 35/km2	220-360
Europe, 17th Century	32-36			Italy, 1650: 37/km2 France, 1650: 38/km2 Belgium, 1650: 50/km2	545
Europe, 18th Century	34-38		30+/km2	"Industrial Revolution" Italy, 1750: 50/km2 France, 1750: 44/km2 Belgium, 1750: 108/km2	720
Massachusetts, 1840		41	90+/km2	Life expectancies: "Industrialized," right; "Pre-industrialized," left	1,200
United Kingdom, 1861		43			
Guatemala, 1893	24				
European Russia, 1896	32				
Czechoslovakia, 1900		40			
Japan, 1899		44			
United States, 1900		48			
Sweden, 1903		53			
France, 1946		62			
India, 1950	41				2,500
Sweden, 1960		73			
1970			**1975**		3,900
United States		71	26/km2		
West Germany		70	248/km2		
Japan		73	297/km2		
China	59		180/km2		
India	48		183/km2		
Belgium			333/km2		

the U.S. Federal Reserve System, which preempt powers which should be reserved to representative agencies of sovereign nation-state republics. The assertion, that a "market" process tends to produce a statistically appropriate money-price, is the babbling of either an economics illiterate, or an outright liar.

The leading political issue, respecting how prices of money and other commodities *should be rigged,* whether by representative agencies of sovereign republics, or by supranational cabals of financier oligarchical interests, is the strategic question: *Which shall reign, sovereign nation-state republics, or "private" financier oligarchies which esteem themselves supranational potencies above governments?*

Under present realities, during which the global system of financier-oligarchy-ruled "free trade," is so visibly in the process of its self-induced disintegration, the proposition before us is clearly nothing other than this: Except for economics illiterates, and liars, the central issue of money-prices is: *How should representative agencies of sovereign nation-state republics "rig markets"?*

This question requires a two-part answer. First, and foremost, the issue is political, and strategic: *How shall we set the conditions determining relative price-movements, to ensure that the republican interest is not weakened to the advantage of humanity's ancient and continuing strategic adversary, the oligarchical interest?* The second leading question is economic: *How shall we regulate the flow of money and credit, to such effect that the "ratio of 'free energy' to 'energy of the system'" does not decline, while promoting scientific and technological progress in the productive powers of labor, through increasing the capital intensity of 'energy of the system,' per capita, per household, and per square kilometer of relevant land-area?* How do we regulate price movements, and credit streams, to ensure that the appropriate physical-economic function is observed in practice? Both questions may then be combined into one: *How is the national economic security (of the perfectly sovereign nation-state republic) best immunized against the two principal epidemics most often fatal to the institutions of human freedom: the diseases of economic devolution, and growth of financier-oligarchical influences?*

The national economic security, is defined, in turn, as the required, not-entropic increase of potential relative population-density, and improved demographic characteristics and standard of living for each and all age and other cohorts of the total population.

The general objective in price policy, is to cheapen relative prices while increasing the productivity, physical income, and demographic characteristics of every part of the labor force, excepting parasitical and redundant functions of administration and finance. (A man as wise as Jonathan Swift might recommend, that the latter economic categories should be culled regularly, and the culls reassigned to honest labor. A modern Rabelais might recommend regular sweeps of Manhattan's Wall Street, and similar gathering-places of both the parasite and Paris-ite classes in every country, to this same salutary purpose.) This accords with such measures as providing a Humboldt grade of universal public education to every child and adolescent, and, increasingly, a comparable higher education of the same quality. It requires a health policy of prolonging life, in defiance of every category of life-impairing affliction, constantly pushing back the boundaries which constrict human life. It requires persisting increase in the capital-intensity and power-intensity, of a productive process driven by investment focussed upon increase of productivity and product types and quality, through priority assigned to investment in scientific and technological progress.

This requires a policy of more abundant and cheaper credit, and more favorable tax-treatment, for those undertakings which accord with this notion of national economic security, and relatively less generous treatment for matters which lie outside these high-priority aspects of the economy. It requires an emphasis upon long-term investment, over short-term, using the same "weapons" of monetary, credit, trade, tariff, and tax policy, to obtain the desired relative movements in prices and credit-flows.

It requires fostering trends in international trade which work to these same goals in relations among sovereign nation-state republics. Relatively fixed parities among national currencies, and low prices of long-term trade, infrastructure-building, and productive-investment credit, over the medium and long term cycles. National food security assured to all nations, and promotion of growth in physical productivity, rather than cheapening of the average price of labor in international trade.

In all, movements in money prices must be orchestrated in such a way as to bring trade, investment, production, and consumption, into patterns of flow which accord with the indicated general metric: not-entropic increase of the potential relative population-density of sovereign nation-state republics, most notably our own. The wise government, when it is able to do so, will rely upon defining the axioms of the economic hypothesis, more, and desire less the direct administration of prices of individual commodities.

Economics: The Subjective Science

A consistent policy of what we today might term "zero technological growth," was the recurring cause for the "dynastic" collapses of all societies organized according to that oligarchical principle typified by the "oligarchical model," the so-called "Babylonian," or "Persian" model of Rome, Byzantium, Venice, and the landed and financier aristocracies of feudal Europe.[57] The "zero technological-growth" policies of the Diocletian Code, were a continuing influence of Byzantium on the reigning internal policies of feudal Europe, until the virtual elimination of the landed aristocracy as a ruling institution, during World War I. It was this same policy, of "zero technological progress," as embedded axiomatically in Diocletian's Code, which brought about the internal, cultural, economic, demographic, and political self-destruction of Byzantine rule, through A.D. 1453, and beyond, to the collapse of the Ottoman Empire during World War I. Any civilization which adopted such a policy of "zero technological progress" (such as today's neo-Malthusian "environmentalism"), was destroyed internally by that policy, and stands, like the poet Percy Bysshe Shelley's fabled *Ozymandias*, a pitiable relic upon the sands of dead history, today.

Why do oligarchical forms of society insist, like a lunatic set upon his self-destruction, on the interrelated policies of "zero technological growth" and "population control," by means of which every great empire of the past destroyed itself from within? Are our modern oligarchs such "lemmings" of the sociologists' animal-experiments laboratories, that they cannot escape their recurring dynastic nightmare, even after so many thousands years? Today, this mass-murderous, but also suicidal species of pervert, insists upon repeating the kind of policies which we may recognize today as the policies of the 1961-founded World Wildlife Fund, created by the arch-oligarchs of the late-Twentieth century, the British Empire's Prince Philip, and Nazi-SS veteran Prince Bernhard of the Netherlands? History, and Prince Philip's own utterances on the matter, like those of the Worldwide Fund for Nature, and kindred institutions, coincide.

There are two, inseparably connected motives.

First, the global oligarchical class which Princes Philip and Bernhard represent in the post-World War II process, have a perverted, totally pagan misconception of human nature, which Prince Philip expresses publicly, repeatedly. He insists on standing out in public, his naked face shamelessly displayed, insisting that he is not a man as *Genesis* and Christianity define man and woman, but something more like a monkey; he insists that he is a "higher ape." He insists that mankind is no better than just another species, whose herds and flocks must be culled, as murderously as might be necessary, to yield managed herds which are more manageable, both in numbers and in down-breeding's selected traits of docility[58]: like selected Hollywood actresses, se-

---

57. The following note is supplied here, as a matter of facts relevant to, and influential today, for the reader's deeper understanding of the present times in which we live today. The term "oligarchical model," as interchangeable with "Persian model," was the currency of mid-Fourth-century B.C. Classical Greece. These usages arose for modern scrutiny, in the negotiations by (the enemies of Socrates and Plato,) the Persian Magi caste, with King Philip of Macedon. This occurred during the time of Aristotle's teacher and controller, the Isocrates who headed the leading school of sophistry in Athens of that time, Isocrates' School of Rhetoric, the same Isocrates who played a conspicuous role in the policy-discussions surrounding the mooted East-West "detente" of that time. As was famously proposed by the Persian Emperor, to King Philip's son and political adversary, Alexander "the Great," this was the "one world" project of that place in history: A "detente" whose intent was to end the centuries-long war between the Persian Empire and the intellectually and militarily superior Greeks, by establishing a division of the Persian Empire, between "West" (west, approximately, of the Halys and Eurphrates rivers), and "East." The Macedonian monarchy was repeatedly offered the hereditary imperial rule over the West, on condition that Macedonia subdue those stubborn Greeks whom the Persians had never developed the wit and military skill to conquer. The added condition was, that the social model of the western empire conform to the oliagrchical model of the Achaemenids. Actually, the "Persian Empire" was nothing but the old Babylonian Empire revitalized under the "hired new management" selected by the ruling families of Babylon, the hereditary priest-caste, akin to the priesthood of the Delphi Cult of Apollo. The model of Mediterranean-wide East-West Empire, was revived, first, during the wars of the First century B.C., in which the Capri agreement between Octavian (Augustus) and the Magi priests of Mithra, established Rome as the capital of a "world empire," and the second phase, under Diocletian, in which the Empire was divided between an eastern and western division, the religious-cultural "balance of power" division of Europe, from the Code of Diocletian, to the present day. It was from these precedents, that the modern British Empire designed the orchestration of the "geopolitical" balance of power between eastern and western Europe, since the beginning of this century, and still attempts to do so, in two World Wars, one Cold War, and the present Anglo-French *Entente Cordiale* manipulation of internal Moscow strategic perceptions and policies, today.

58. In his 1923 *The Prospects of Industrial Civilization*, the Hitler-like Bertrand Russell supplied an utterance typical of him, and the "Jenny" of Bertolt Brecht's *Three-Penny Opera* script: "… the white population of the world will soon cease to increase. The Asiatic races will be longer, and the negroes still longer, before their birth rate falls sufficiently to

lected like races of dogs, for breeding-stock, not for brains and character of the progeny ("Zeus save us!"), but for the down-bred qualities of fancied pulchritude, as preferred by the current crop of judges at the eugenics breeding marathons.

Second, it has penetrated even the sun-drenched, Gila-Monster-like, sluggish wits of these oligarchs, that the mere existence of the modern sovereign nation-state republic, is a menace to future world-rule by the oligarchical species. It has occurred to even these high-ranking spokesmen of the Brutish Empire, that the uplifting of the ninety-five percent of humanity, from their imperial status as virtual human cattle, to persons enjoying a universal cognitive quality of education, and the opportunity to participate in the benefits of generalized scientific and technological progress, produces a quality of individual, economically and in every other way, which is vastly superior to the typical member of a society ruled by "free trade" and pro-Malthusian ideologies of practice. It is also apparent to, and explicitly desired by, a well-tanned specimen like Prince Philip, that without that design of modern nation-state republic set into motion by Dante Alighieri, Nicolaus of Cusa, the A.D. 1439-1440 sessions of the Council of Florence, and the A.D. 1461-1483 establishment of the first such state by France's Louis XI, the condition of approximately ninety-five percent of humanity will fall back, without visible hope of repair, to the status of human cattle. Witness the persisting pattern, since the 1960's, of the degeneration of children of formerly human subjects of Her Majesty, once capable, in pre-Harold Wilson days, of the cognitive functions of modern industrial labor, to such pathetic "Yahoos" as England's homicidal, beast-like football fanatics of the 1970's, and, worse, today.

That, in a capsule, is what the row is all about. All of

---

make their numbers stable without help of war and pestilence…. Until that happens, the benefits aimed at by socialism can only be partially realized, and the less prolific races will have to defend themselves against the more prolific by methods which are disgusting even if they are necessary." Russell's is the same mentality exhibited by the later Averell Harriman and President George Bush's father, Prescott, in their leading role in supporting Hitler's London-orchestrated, 1933 accession to power in Germany. This is the oligarchical culture of Sparta in the Delphi Apollo-cult tradition of Lycurgus, and the tradition of the pagan empires of Babylon, and Rome. Bertrand Russell, Averell Harriman, Prescott Bush, *et al.*, are merely typical of the bloody face of oligarchism. These are representatives, by enculturation, of a sub-human, predatory species, against which civilization must defend itself, by methods which are necessary, but by no means "disgusting."

the other topics of European history since the Fifteenth century, and all of world history since the Eighteenth century, are merely incidental matters of secondary or much less importance, than this one conflict, between republicanism and oligarchism, humanist Renaissance versus financier-oligarchical Enlightenment. This row is the single, overriding issue of all history, all national policy, of every nation, today. Who does not acknowledge that fact, knows nothing of real politics anywhere today.

The capital penalties prescribed for offenses against the Malthusian features of Diocletian's code, illustrate the point. The characteristic of an oligarchical model of society, is the condemnation of approximately ninety-five percent of the population to what is sometimes identified as a "traditional society," in which each is prescribed as doing now what his, or her father or mother did before. The fact is, that today's so-called "environmental" codes are largely outright hoaxes, like the fraudulent banning of DDT by Environmental Protection Agency Administrator William Ruckelshaus, the multi-layered fraud of F. Sherwood Rowland's argument for banning of CFC's, "Global Warming," and so on. The fact that most of the policies associated with the Worldwide Fund for Nature, Greenpeace, and so forth, are anti-scientific frauds, is neither unknown, nor of concern to the financier oligarchy circles which deploy these organizations top-down.

It is really simple to understand why the oligarchs do this: To manage minds, as much as sizes of human populations, by Bertrand Russell's methods, which oligarchs deem "necessary, even if they are disgusting." Dupe credulous, ignorant graduates of today's "politically correct" universities and secondary schools, to put on their shackles and lock themselves into their pens each night, by luring them to believe what the oligarchs since time immemorial have always demanded that the duped human cattle of society believe, even on pain of death for the non-believer, death administered to the accompanying approbation, and Malthusian baas and bellows, of the credulous cattle themselves.

The environmentalist's technologically fixed mode of human behavior, is itself the mental condition natural to beasts, not human beings. It is the mentality imposed upon the slave, and serf, and wrought upon the tens of thousands of victims of living human sacrifice by the worse-than-Nazi Aztecs. It is the mentality which prompts that victim to make himself a slave or serf, or a man helplessly awaiting his own sacrifice upon the

Cancel the British System, Save the People   63

Aztec altar, until some event, such as a Cortez, might come to lead the victims to triumph over the bestial oppressors. It is the imprisonment of the human mind within illiteracy, which defines the slave, that slave-like mentality which knows no better that to preserve a "traditional society," a society based upon a technologically fixed theorem-lattice of human knowledge and behavior.

It is in this light, that one must understand the "why" of the essential incompetence of virtually every accepted doctrine of economics taught in any university of this planet today, the bestiality of John Von Neumann's "n-person, zero-sum game" of economy, included most emphatically in this roster of academic charlatanry. There is no mankind in that economics. Where in what passes for a functional principle in their scheme, do we find the principle of valid, axiomatic-revolutionary discovery of natural principle as a "causal" factor in determining the outcome of policies of economic practice? Perhaps it is because the economics taught in our universities and textbooks is so obscenely absurd, that a blushing Lemuel Gulliver preferred to protect tender minds from knowing that such depraved doctrines were practised among the academicians of Laputa. "That stuff," to give it its strictly proper scientific name, was never intended ("Zeus forbid!") to be scientific, even rational. It was never intended to be other than a superstition, to be induced among the credulous. It was never intended to be other than a lunatic ideology, like that which John Maynard Keynes encountered, when he opened the chest of papers from Isaac Newton's laboratory.

Bat's wing, and eye of newt, with a bit of the cabala thrown into the recipe; ("Samiel be adored!") There, in that fabulously stinking witch's pot, is all there is to be learned of economics from the devotees of Faust, Mandeville, Smith, and Johnny Von Neumann.

Once we have situated the problem of taught economics as being the control which the oligarchical class exerts over our markets and our universities, once we know what the row is all about, we have isolated the internal problem of formalities to the degree it then may be addressed as a scientific matter.

Where in the formal mathematics of Galileo, Descartes, Newton, Euler, Helmholtz, or Bertrand Russell, is the place where the action of valid discovery of principle may be placed, to define the characteristic feature of economy? Nowhere? The place exists, but that crack has been bulldozed over, hidden for a moment by the malicious intent of the "sliding rule," Euler's referenced tautological fallacy. The principle, is Leibniz's *monad*; the place, is the mathematical discontinuities in the fabric of the formalist's physical space-time. The key, is Leibniz's attack on the efforts of Clarke and poor Newton to defend the fraudulent claim, that the calculus could be represented by means of the kind of infinite series derived from an Aristotelean, Cartesian misreading of Euclid's *Elements*. The answer is supplied by study of those densely packed mathematical discontinuities, which riddle, like sea-worms, the pillars of Euler's vitual-reality edifice. Thus, for the present author, the *Monadology,* with the *Leibniz-Clarke Correspondence,* supplied the pivot, on which the refutation of Wiener's statistical absurdity turned.[59]

Repeated successes, in validating axiomatic-revolutionary qualities of discovery of physical principle, prove conclusively, that cognition, whose knowable existence Aristotle, empiricism, and Immanuel Kant deny, exists. The increase in man's power over nature, *per capita,* demonstrates that that cognitive act is efficient. The presence of cognition, as something not captured by any mathematical schema, can be demonstrated. The efficiency of cognition is also demonstrable. The remaining challenge becomes, "How can the act of cognition itself be known, in a sense comparable to knowledge of a sense-perception?" Here, Classical art-forms take over the highest prominences of scientific method.

There are two preconditions to be satisfied, before a Platonic idea can be realized with that quality of immediacy less literate folk associate with "sense certainty." First, immediacy relies upon emotion, erotic or agapic. Without the arousal of the agapic sense of passion for truth, there is no verisimilitude to that Platonic idea of principle, even though the experimental proof of the principle's existence is complete. This sense of verisimilitude is evoked in science in the same manner it is aroused by well-composed examples of Classical art-forms. That arousal can occur only in the same way that the relevant ancient Greek literature, from the Homeric epics, through the dialogues of Plato evoke the presence of *agapē,* as we have touched upon this matter here, as in earlier locations. Now, the present author takes the liberty of "plagiarizing himself," excerpting a passage of several pages duration from a document which he produced earlier this year. It is a portion of

____

59. References are supplied in footnote 1.

that earlier document which addresses the specific matter immediately before us here. In the following excerpt, the author elicits the relevant, common features of three types of ancient Greek literature: Homeric epic, Classical tragedy of Athens' "Golden Age," and Plato's Socratic dialogues.

The excerpt begins:

Look at the three, identified types of Classical-Greek literature from the vantage-point of these observations on the subject of theorem-lattices. Treat each of these types of literature from the vantage-point of that Classical-Greek notion of hypothesis adopted by Riemann.

The type of subject-matter to which the Homeric epics are devoted, is the interconnected relationships among gods, the human individual, and nature. The themes of these epics—the interconnected struggles among gods, man, and nature, are the most frequent points of reference for the later tragedies of Greece's "Golden Age" authors. In turn, the method of the Classical tragedies is the point of reference for Plato's development of the method of his Socratic dialogues, the same *method of hypothesis* employed by Riemann for the physics of his 1854 habilitation dissertation. The problem posed by the negotiations of a new world monetary order among the four world powers, is of a type already implicit in the problem of differing hypotheses, as between gods and man, in the Homeric epics.

For this comparison, the relevant case is the instance in which the fabled gods and some mortals, from the epics, experience the self-same event, but react differently to it.[60] This type of case appears again in the tragedies, and, in a slightly different, but derived form, in Plato's Socratic dialogues.[61]

This kind of difference in reaction, is not to be regarded as simply a difference in the interpretation of an event shared in common. We must read these differences in the sense of an efficient (e.g., physical) interaction between two mutually inconsistent processes, two incompatible physical geometries.

The one—man, or god—sharing the same event, does not merely generate a different sense-perception of the common event; the physical acts he makes in response to the stimulus of that event, will be different in its effect on man and nature than the reaction of the other. As we shall see, this notion of variability of practical, willful responses to the same events, is the essence of the science of physical economy.

The difference between the mortal man and the god, as this occurs in Homeric epic or Classical tragedy, is premised upon differences in the underlying, axiomatic quality of assumptions of each, with respect to the other. As a pedagogical ruse here, examine the sequences of developments in a simplified, schematic way.

The man reacts to the event, by attempting to formulate a proposition which is consistent with his axiomatic notions respecting the character of the relations among gods, mortals, and nature. The god reacts analogously, excepting the fact that his axiomatic assumptions differ from those of the man. Each, then tends to refine his tentative propositions to the effect of eliminating inconsistencies with the relevant underlying set of axioms and postulates. The resulting proposition, in each case, then constitutes either a theorem of that theorem-lattice, or an approximation of such a theorem.

Therefore, in respect to formalities, the respective theorems of the god and the mortal will be mutually inconsistent. In respect to physics, the impact of the resulting action upon the physical universe by the man, will be of a correspondingly different character than the impact of the action by the god.

Thus, the dramatic appreciation of a Classical Greek epic, or tragedy, presents to us combinations of charac-

---

60. E.g., Aeschylos' *Prometheus Bound.* In this tragedy, the false presumption of Zeus and his Olympus cronies, is that torture dictates it to be in Prometheus' self-interest to reveal to Zeus the deadly secret of Zeus' doom. Prometheus is operating on different axioms than Zeus *et al.*; his concern is to save his own life's work, the protection and development of mankind; Zeus is committed to the elimination of the human species. Thus, Prometheus' self-interest dictates that he must not provide Zeus any information which might result in Zeus' escaping the common doom of the gods of Olympus; the good Prometheus, by keeping the secret, even at the price of prolonged torment, will triumph over the evil Zeus. Similarly, shallow-minded commentators assume that the Prometheus of this play is a tragic figure, when the subject of the drama is, most plainly, the tragic doom of Zeus! Zeus' Olympians, the archetypes of oligarchical evil deploying capricious whims against mankind, are doomed because they insist on remaining the oligarchy they are: not a conception willingly received by the decadent dons of Oxbridge.

61. The approach we are employing here, illustrates the importance of the adolescent student's familiarity with the art and science of Classical Greece, in preparing the student to become qualified as a statesman, scientist, or even as a true citizen. If we are alert to what we are studying, we find embedded in the seemingly homely entertainments from Classical Greek tradition, the distinct notions to which the highest forms of artistic and scientific thought today owe much. Often, the modern translator has buried these crucial subtleties from sight, by means of a gloss which is either simply slovenly, or an ideologically motivated misrepresentation. These Classical works must be studied with regard for what is not to be overlooked, that which appears in the corner of one's mind's eye.

ters, or clusters of characters, which are each of a distinct type. That is to say, they are each representative of a distinct hypothesis.

One might illustrate the same point respecting Greek art, by imagining the case of three characters from ancient Greece: one from Sparta (of the type of Lycurgus' tradition), another from Athens (of the type of Solon's tradition),[62] and a third, mutually detested by all three, from Thebes. Each represents a different hypothesis; in the case of a commonly experienced event, each formulates propositions differently than the other two, and the efficient actions taken in response to each of the respective propositions, will have a different physical effect than the actions of each of the remaining two.

The notion of hypothesis pertains not merely to differences among hypotheses; that elaboration of the principled notion of hypothesis, which we have acquired from Plato, demands that we define a fixed hypotheses in respect to the manner in which the hypothesis of the individual type may be changed. The existence of an efficient science of physical economy depends absolutely upon this notion of *change*.

Modern science thus begins with those later Plato dialogues which his *Parmenides* implicitly serves as prologue; that "ontological paradox" which Plato identifies as the proof of the fallacy of the Eleatics' (e.g., Parmenides') reductionist-formalist method, is located in the Eleatics' refusal to consider those implications of the notion of change, by means of which the proof of the notion of hypothesis may be accessed.[63] Plato's so-

lution, in his sundry later dialogues, for that "ontological paradox" exposed by the *Parmenides,* is the notion of hypothesis employed by Riemann.

To wit: As Riemann's habilitation dissertation exemplifies this argument, *the principle upon which modern experimental physics and analogous science depends, is the presumption that there exists an implicitly measurable demonstration, that each valid, revolutionary discovery of new physical principle, increases the power of the human species over nature, per capita and per square kilometer of relevant land-area of our planet.* That argument is the empirical principle under which the notions of the rational human individual, and of science, are subsumed. To wit: *the notion that reason may resolve differences in hypothesis, presumes that all normal human beings are born with the potential for assimilating ideas corresponding to an orderable sequence of progress in increase of the potential productive powers of labor, per capita, per family household, and per square kilometer of relevant land-area employed. On this basis, and no other basis, there exists a quality of knowable truth, the which is independent of, and superior to any set of extant opinions.*[64]

Knowledge of such a science of history, did not end with the Greeks. This is the subject of Friedrich Schiller's discussion of the relationship between his own stage tragedies and those of William Shakespeare. To illustrate the point respecting *change,* witness the most celebrated passage from *Hamlet*: the following excerpt from Hamlet's soliloquy near the beginning of Act III.

> ... The undiscovered country, from whose bourn
> No traveller returns, —puzzles the will,
> And makes us rather bear those ills we have
> Than fly to others that we know not of.
> Thus conscience doth make cowards of us all;

---

62. The allusion here, is to Friedrich Schiller's treatment of the contrast between the legislation of Solon and Lycurgus.

63. This argument is illustrated by the case of Riemann's ridiculing of Isaac Newton's "*et hypotheses non fingo…*": "*Das Trägheitsgesetz ist die Hypothese: Wenn ein materieller Punkt allein in der Welt vorhanden wäre und sich in Raum mit einer bestimmten Geschwindigkeit bewegte, so würde er diese Geschwingdigkeit beständig behalten.*" *Werke*, pp. 524-525. Compare the comment on Newton with the opening argument of Riemann's habilitation dissertation (subtitled *Plan der Untersuchung*), op cit., pp. 272-273. Only by considering the changes in the axiomatic notions of space-time which are imposed by introducing the matter of the empirical relations, is the conditional (e.g., hypothetical) nature of our assumptions respecting space-time forced to our attention. The general principle to be adduced, is not found merely by considering objects of naive sense-perception; it demands treating as objects of thought, those kinds of relations in physical space-time which are shown to be measurably efficient, principled forms of relations, but relations of a type which do not exist for us as independently perceptible objects of the senses. [*Cf.* Riemann, "*I. Zur Psychologie und Metaphysik,*" *Werke,* pp. 509-520. See, also, Lyndon H. LaRouche, Jr. on Riemann's use of *Geistesmassen* as a technical term, in LaRouche, "On The Subject of Metaphor," *Fidelio,* Vol. 1, No. 3, Fall 1992.] Iso-

chronism, for example, is not an object of the senses; contrary to the pathological presumptions of some, it is not a "property" of the cycloid. Rather, as Bernoulli *et al.* demonstrated, the existence of the cycloid is determined by material relations characteristic of physical space-time in general: geometry does not determine physical space-time, but, rather, our progress in discovering improved hypotheses respecting efficient relations within physical space-time, determines our always imperfect ideas respecting geometry.

64. This does not signify that the ordering can be predetermined in any sense other than "greater than/less than." The idea that there might exist an *a priori* formal geometry for comparing orderings of the $(n+1)/n$ type by the yardstick of "linearization in the very small," is as absurd a notion as it is a somewhat popularized, and arbitrary one.

And thus the native hue of resolution
Is sicklied over with the pale cast of thought;
And enterprises of great pith and moment,
With this regard, their currents turn awry,
And lose the name of action."[65]

Rather bear those ills we have," our presently adopted hypothesis, rather "than fly to others," a new hypothesis, "that we know not of." A persisting refusal to effect that change in hypothesis, by means of which latter we might survive the assured doom of clinging to our old hypothesis, is the essence of the way in which great empires expire through dynastic catastrophe; they are doomed not so much by their palpable adversaries, as by their own fatal devotion to "our traditions." Exactly so, did that swaggering butcher, Hamlet, bring himself to the doom, over which carnage Shakespeare's Horatio said in Act V:

> ... give order that these bodies
> High on stage be placed to view;
> And let me speak to the yet unknowing world
> How these things came about:
>
> ...
>
> And, in this upshot, purposes mistook
> Fallen upon the inventors' heads: All this can I
> Truly deliver.
>
> ...
>
> But let this same be presently performed,
> Even while men's minds are wild: lest more
>   mischance
> On plots and errors happen.

Doom falls often upon those who suffer the special cowardice common among history's bloody-bladed soldiers. One speaks of bold men, like the swashbuckling Hamlet, "the good old boy," who was struck down, bloodily, by nothing so much as his own terror in face of

an idea contrary to his accustomed beliefs. One may speak, so, of the cowardice of the football hero (like Zeus, that bullying, doomed wretch of *Prometheus Bound*), who, away from his accustomed play, finds himself cursed by a world whose reality now defies his infantile rules of sport. Like the contemptible Zeus, the Hamlets of real life may blame Fate, but, the truth of the matter is, that each of these swaggering victims has doomed himself to a mewling end; the instrument of his self-undoing is his peculiar terror in face of ideas which, to him, are strange. In the end, history always cheats such blockheaded bully-boys; to such effect, history, time and time again, changes abruptly the rules of play. So, Hamlet and his kind, like the Eleatics, sophists, and rhetoricians after Parmenides, would rather die than accept the principle of Heraclitus and Plato, that nothing within this mortal's world is fundamental, but change itself.

That attribution of change, is not a plaything of artistic elegance; it is the cornerstone of all scientific truth. To the point: If the three crucial world powers, the U.S.A., Russia, and China, were to reject an effective basis for common agreement on a new, just world economic order established jointly by means of their leadership, this planet would, like Hamlet, be plunged quickly into the worst dark age in history. Specifically, were they, like the tragic Hamlet, to allow themselves to fall back into defending "our traditions," rather than find a new, common, scientific solution, the implosive collapse of the world monetary-financial system could not be averted longer than the short-term; then, the collapse of a now highly interdependent system of world economy would unleash the worst, accelerating, downward spiral of famine, disease, and related homicidal strife throughout the planet as a whole.

If those world powers retreated, each like the self-doomed Hamlet, into clinging to the argument of "our traditions"—"rather bear those ills we have, than fly to others that we know not of," all existing nations, including those powers, would soon become politically extinct in the demographic holocaust into which their stubborn false pride had lured them. In this "dynastic crisis," this virtual "Twilight of the Gods," not only would most of today's existing lesser powers evaporate from the political map; many would become also biologically extinct, as the world's potential population-density were driven, rapidly, down toward levels not exceeding the approximate three hundred millions individuals populating this planet during the time of Europe's Fourteenth century. That is not fantasy, not con-

---

65. The U.S.A. of 1861-1865 enjoyed the benefit of two extraordinary commanders. Notable was the William Tecumseh Sherman (the "Anvil" of the Grant-Sherman pair) whose genius was highlighted by Alfred v. Schlieffen's *Cannæ*. The greater genius of these two Americans, was Sherman's commander-in-chief, President Abraham Lincoln, who shaped much of the policy of the U.S.A.'s struggle against Britain's diabolical creation, the Confederacy, with aid of lessons from Shakespeare's dramas. The decisive role, during 1863, of Russia's alliance with Lincoln against the Victorian Britain of Palmerston, Russell, and the "Black Age's" Prince Albert Edward, renders the reference to Sherman and Lincoln of double significance in the setting of the present writing.

jecture; it is a straightforward scientific calculation.

For today's nations to live, they—especially the indicated three world powers—must have the courage and wisdom to change, to depart the Hamlet-like "traditions" which presently augur their doom.

The excerpt ends there.

In all Classical art-forms, as in this indicated connection among epic, tragedy, and Socratic dialogue, the same active principle operates. Around a subject, which has a sensuous component attracting some interest, a problem is defined. The problem's solution is shown to center in the needed resolution of a conflict among several hypotheses. In the Classical Greek epic, tragedy, and Socratic dialogue, the relevant hypotheses are represented by characters, or groups of characters. In all cases, any prospective hero's solution to the problem, such as the Ulysses of the *Odyssey,* or Zeus, the anti-hero of Aeschylos' *Prometheus Bound,* must solve something akin to a riddle. The solution requires insight, not into the mere opinions of the other characters, but, rather, perception of the hypotheses which underlie the generation of their respective theorem-lattices of opinion. Usually the character which might pass for prospective hero, or anti-hero, can solve the riddle only by changing his own hypothesis, as key to mastering the effects of the hypotheses of the others.

It is not so difficult to recognize the carry-over of the same principle, from Classical poetry and drama, into the Classical *lied* of Mozart, Beethoven, Schubert, Brahms, *et al.* The counterpoint of that motivic thorough-composed form of song, might help to open up the more general principles of Classical vocal polyphony, and, hence, to adduce more readily the Socratic dialogue of Classical thorough-composition in general. Understanding the Classical principle of artistic composition, so, in epic, drama, dialogue, poetry, and music, trains the mind's eye to seek the same principle of Socratic dialogue at the core of the plastic art-form.

The characteristic features of the Classical artistic experience are centered in two aspects of the matter.

First, the method of the Socratic dialogue, focuses attention upon the process of thinking, rather than the thought-product, focuses upon the hypothesis, rather than the mere theorem. There is more. The hypothesis must be considered as a subject of change; it is the prospect of changing an hypothesis, as a method of solving a problem otherwise insoluble, which is key to the function of the Socratic dialogue. Thus, the *monad* comes to the fore; it is *change* which is the quality of the indivis-ible *monad,* change from nothing less than from one hypothesis to another. Thus, the substance of the *monad* is the quality of *higher hypothesis.* This, the ontological quality of the higher hypothesis, is the quality of the singularity which resolves a competently defined formal discontinuity in a mathematical-physical process, for example.

Second, the method of the Socratic dialogue, is the only means by which a person might render his own mental processes the subject of *efficient consciousness.* By looking deeply enough into the mind of others, by focussing upon the hypotheses underlying their thinking processes, one is enabled to cause them, if only in one's own imagination, to become conscious of one's own thinking processes. Through that feat of the imagination, employed as a mirror, one may render one's own conscious processes the subject of a sense of immediacy, and willful attention.

That precisely, is the essential function of all Classical art. To see, through media typified by the common features of Homeric epic, Classical tragedy, and Socratic dialogue, how the thinking processes of men and women are transformed to the effect of solving problems which could not be solved if each clung, like some race of dog, to his or her own, as if hereditarily predetermined hypothesis. Above all, to employ art so contrived to enable one to become efficiently conscious of the power to change one's own hypothesis willfully, to this purpose.

When one has learned great discoveries from the past, by the method of reenacting the act of original discovery in one's own mind, a corresponding moment of the mental life of the original discoverer comes to reside in one's own mind. In this fashion, the properly educated student not only populates his, or her mind with the living personalities of important original discoverers; the student acquires the habit of developing such relations with others, living and deceased alike, throughout later life. The mind of the properly educated person comes alive with a great dialogue of the type suggested by Raphael Sanzio's famous mural, *The School of Athens.* In moments seized by a relevant topic, that person's mind comes alive with a dialogue among the assembled, remembered minds of the discoverers who have come to take up residence there. In reading Riemann's habilitation dissertation, one can almost hear their voices, as Riemann summons them to the foreground of his argument. When Riemann writes on the topic of *Geistesmassen,* in his posthumously published *Zur Psychologie und Metaphysik,* one can sense the nearby presence of Leibniz speaking on the subject of the *monad,* or anticipate the present author's writing on the subject of *metaphor* to kindred effect. The dialogue is science, but it is a science ruled by the Classical art-form of Homeric epic, Aeschylean tragedy, and Socratic dialogue, as all true science must be.

It is the ability to develop an agapic functional sense of immediacy respecting the Leibniz *monad,* the act of higher hypothesis, which is the essential difference between the scientifically impotent follower of Aristotle, and the fruitful scientific worker. It is in the special, agapic passions which the methods of dialogue underlying great Classical art arouse, that Classical art functions as the precondition for effective science, that art reveals itself as the highest expression of science. It is through such art, and that alone, that the immediacy of what Leibniz identifies as the *monad* is rendered efficiently intelligible.

Finally: Man Rules The Universe, By Pre-Design

By the nature of the accomplishment, that mankind's successful increase of its potential relative population-density, occurs through valid axiomatic-revolutionary discoveries of principle, acts of discovery which lie outside the domain of any formal mathematics, there is no formal mathematical proof, or disproof of the mental activity by means of which a succession of such valid discoveries is ordered. Rather, *that a measurable advancement is ordered by this means, shows that the principle expressed by such a succession of discoveries, is itself in harmony with a deep principle of design of the universe as a whole.* Human existence, taken as a whole, is "the great experiment," upon which certainty of scientific principles ultimately depends.

In Plato's argument, what we have just stated, as we had announced this earlier, here, points to the interaction between the *monad* identifiable as *hypothesizing the higher hypothesis* and the highest *monad,* the ultimate *Good.* The *Good,* the "alpha and omega" of the universe's existence, does not change, but, rather changes that which acts upon it. From moment to moment, the *higher hypothesis* acts as a relative "alpha and omega" to the changes in hypothesis which it orders, as a simple hypothesis is the relative "alpha and omega" to the theorem-lattice it subsumes. So, the act of *hypothesizing the higher hypothesis* subsumes the succession of changes in higher hypothesis. Thus, we

have man revealed as made in the image of the Creator, by virtue of this power for valid changes in hypothesis, for that *measurably efficient* principle of change which lies outside, and above any possible mathematical schema. This all sorts itself out, once we learn to look at the matter from the appropriate perspective.

The key is the notion of "universal characteristics."

For example, the characteristic of all valid axiomatic-revolutionary discovery of principle, is an ordering of human existence which satisfies the not-entropic metric, which was expressed in approximation here, as the requirement that the ratio of "free energy" to "energy of the system" not decline, although the "energy of system" *per capita, per* household, and *per* square kilometer must increase in absolute physical terms of measure. All successful discovery of changes in economic and related policy satisfy that requirement. That that requirement has been satisfied to the degree history demonstrates, shows that the creative principle of the individual human mind, the principle of higher hypothesis, generates an interaction with the universe which has the effect of "not-entropy." Thus, the principle of not-entropy, so expressed, is the most fundamental principle of our knowledge of the universe as a whole.

The subsidiary point, derived from that same argument, is that "not-entropy" is *the universal characteristic* of the power of higher hypothesis (and hypothesizing the higher hypothesis). This is a characteristic of the relationship between that individual power of hypothesis and the universe.

That relationship also expresses, in the sense of "alpha and omega," the relationship of the individual person's existence to the universe, and to all past and future mankind.

We are each, in our brief mortal existence, the repository of that which is given to us, life, and culture, above all the rest. Because we are human, we are creatures of ideas, rather than mere biological heredity. The ideas we acquire, are products of those principles which we have assimilated from our society by reenacting the relevant act of discovery within our mental processes. We are thus joined immediately to discoverers who lived millennia and centuries before us, more closely than most of our next-door neighors. If we preserve that talent afforded to us, and seek to improve the gift of life and knowledge which we pass on to others, we may conclude an unquestionably necessary individual life, which will have been, in its fashion, a boon to society centuries and millennia after we have died.

Then, in that distant future time, the hypotheses we have known will be as an earlier century's long fallen dead leaves. Yet, the process of hypothesizing the higher hypothesis, the process to which we have contributed our part in our time, lives on, as a *monad* should, and our work thus within it. By recognizing that, we may allow even the distant future to flow into our judgment, and let it shape our choice of present action, today. Whereas the man who but reacts to the present moment, and its pains and satisfactions, is as one who never lived, before or after that ephemeral present moment, with which his existence, like the mayfly's, is scarcely born and already dead.

The transmission of ideas does not occur through a literal reading of words, as if according to their dictionary meanings, nor by means of any other deductive extraction from the composition of sentences and paragraphs. It occurs only "between the cracks" of the literal utterance, as the emergence of ideas is reflected only in those discontinuities in the mathematical-physics fabric which Euler fraudulently denied to exist, as did Immanuel Kant after him. It occurs only through irony. No idea of principle can be communicated by spoken or written language, except by metaphor. Singularities arising in the locus of discontinuities of the mathematical-physics fabric, are the form in which metaphors appear in the language of mathematics.

The communication of ideas of principle—Platonic ideas, can occur only within the sovereign precincts of the individual mind's cognitive processes, and never within the channels of communication as such. It is in the "decoding" of the metaphors appearing in the channels of communication, that a metaphor uttered by one person is decoded, to extract its Platonic ideas, by another. Exemplary is the replication of the act of original, valid, axiomatic-revolutionary principle of nature. This decoding takes the form of a change of hypothesis (i.e., a *monad*), and also the discernment of a "universal characteristic" associated with that changed hypothesis.

Thus, are the ideas produced by the cognitive processes of one from even the distant past, become an integral part of the knowledge of a person in the present. So, do those from the present, transmit the heritage of human knowledge, from both present and past, into the individual cognitive processes of those of future generations. So, in this, and in no other possible way, are the generations of mankind, past, present, and future, bound together as one.

In this same way, we know the future. We have efficient knowledge of the future, to the degree we know those characteristics of the future implicit in the choices of hypothesis upon which we choose to act in the present. It is by choosing among the characteristics represented by choice of hypothesis, that that predetermination is made efficient, and that we become accountable for the future consequences of the commissions and omissions of choice we make today.

If we recognize the universal characteristic of that skein of human progress to which we are committed, we have, in that, the guidance we require, to reach the future, through the efficient reflection of the future upon the present. Conclude with the savor of that thought, as the present author presents, once again, that picture of productive economy which he used to show, in his one-semester classes, under the rubric, "The world-wide cup of coffee."

Every local act of production, today, has efficient antecedents in the past. Materials and products formerly produced, development of land-area and workplace, and relevant basic economic infrastructure previously developed and maintained, and development of persons and their ideas, are all present requirements embodied, from the past, in the present act of production. Similarly, the decision to produce tomorrow, is made in significant degree today. Investments in plant and equipment, for example, have an estimatable "half life" reaching five, seven, or more years into the future: thus, what we decide and do today, mortgages future possibilities.

For example, if we trace out the succession of antecedent bills of materials of every stage of origin of the components of a simple cup of coffee served in a restaurant, taking into account the investment in the facilities employed there, the support of the persons who prepare and serve that coffee, and the materials of the cup and saucer, milk, spoon, sugar, napkin, table, and chair, and also the means by which we were conveyed to that place, that simple cup of coffee reaches around the planet, many times, into the distant past. Look again, at that cup of coffee; think, then, what it means to be human.

The Greek *Prometheus,* "Foresight," must triumph over the wicked oligarchical families who rule Zeus's Olympus. Ideas, and the foresight inhering in the metaphorical process by means of which ideas are developed and transmitted into practice of present and future generations, are the essence of that which distinguishes man, as *Genesis* and the *New Testament* define man and woman. That is, in larger degree than from anyone else in modern times, our heritage from Leibniz. That is the heritage of the science of physical economy.